CITIES OF PRIDE

Also available from Cassell

P. Ainley: *Class and Skill*
P. Alheit: *Taking the Knocks*
D. Atkinson: *Radical Urban Solutions*
M. Barber: *The Making of the 1944 Education Act*
M. Barber: *Education in the Capital*
M. Barber: *Raising Educational Standards in the Inner Cities*
M. Bottery: *Lessons for Schools?*
N. Coggans and S. McKellar: *The Facts about Alcohol,
Aggression and Adolescence*
A. Hargreaves: *Changing Teachers, Changing Times*
I. Lawrence (ed.): *Education Tomorrow*
P. Lunneborg: *OU Women*
P. Mizen: *The State, Young People and Training*
J. Samoff (ed.): *Coping with Crisis*
D. Scott: *Accountability and Control in Educational Settings*

CITIES OF PRIDE

Rebuilding Community, Refocusing Government

Edited by Dr Dick Atkinson

CASSELL

Cassell
Wellington House, 125 Strand, London WC2R 0BB.
215 Park Avenue South, New York, NY 10003, USA.

© Dick Atkinson and the contributors 1995

British Library Cataloguing-in-Publication Data
A catalogue record for this book is available from the British Library.

ISBN 0–304–33403–0 (hardback)
0–304–33404–9 (paperback)

Typeset by Falcon
Printed and bound in Great Britain by
Redwood Books, Trowbridge, Wiltshire

CONTENTS

CONTRIBUTORS

Dick Atkinson   *Director, The Phoenix Centre*
Bob Tyrell   *Director, The Henley Centre*
Charles Handy   *Author and teacher*
Frank Field   *MP, Labour*
Amitai Etzioni   *George Washington University*
Anita Halliday   *St Paul's Community Trust*
John Rennie   *Director, CEDC*
Chris Wadhams   *Director, Wadhams Associates*
Carl Chinn   *Birmingham University*
Joe Holyoak   *Axis Design*
Inger Boyett and Don Finlay   *Nottingham University*
Usha Prashar   *Consultant and Part Director, National Council for Voluntary Service*
Ian Morrison   *Director, Birmingham Voluntary Service Council*
Karin Jacobson   *DUSCO UK*
David Grayson   *Business in the Community*
David Gee   *Environmentalist*
Henry Tam   *St Edmundsbury Council*
Paddy Ashdown   *MP, Leader Liberal Democrats*
Gordon Brown   *MP, Shadow Chancellor*
Alan Howarth   *MP, Conservative*

ACKNOWLEDGEMENTS

Very many people have had a hand in the preparation of this book, either directly by contributing to it or, indirectly, by helping with ideas and discussions or through supporting the 'Cities of Pride' conference held in Birmingham in November 1994, which helped to focus all our thoughts and energies. The need to capture and discuss the common sense of community and its implications for the reorganization of both local and central government has become more and more pressing in recent months and years. Senior politicians have made bolder and better attempts to address the two sides of this coin and to learn from practitioners in the field. Consequently it seemed important to involve as many of these people as possible, culminating first in a series of discussions, then through my DEMOS publication, *The Common Sense of Community*, followed by the Birmingham conference and the national community network which it proposed and, finally, through this book.

While the people and agencies who have helped in this ongoing and developing project, particularly with this book, are too numerous to mention, some stand out. A particular debt is owed to St Paul's, the Birmingham Settlement, Birmingham Council for Voluntary Service, DEMOS, Business in the Community, and Common Purpose for sponsoring the conference and to Matthew Boulton College for financially underwriting it. The conference helped many of us to further develop our ideas and the way we relate to each other. Ian Morrison, Pat Conaty, Jenny Talbot, Karen Kennaby, Suzanne O'Connor, Sir Adrian Cadbury, Sir Richard Knowles and Alan Fitzpatrick are all local Birmingham and Midlands people whose help and advice proved invaluable. In particular, Chris Wadhams of Wadhams Associates was indispensable. Neither conference nor book would have been possible without his encouragement and support as well as that of his wife, Theresa.

Geoff Mulgan, Bob Rowthorn, Melanie Phillips, Henry Tam, Usha Prashar, Tricia Zipfell, Karin Jacobson, Dik Dusseldorp, John Rennie, David Gee, Bob Tyrell and David Grayson have helped in countless ways, especially with ideas and advice. Frank Field, Alan Howarth and Anthony Coombs readily gave invaluable support and helped, along with Charles Handy and Amitai Etzioni, to keep the project afloat when I thought it might be sinking. I am also indebted to Alan Lewis for much typing and layout work. Above all, however, I am grateful to my wife Gill, and children Sophie and Jane for putting up with all the difficulties which the preparation of both the conference and this book imposed upon them. To them, all those mentioned above, and to so many who are not mentioned, I am very grateful. The best contributions and ideas are theirs, the mistakes in editing those ideas are mine alone.

INTRODUCTION

Dick Atkinson

The older generation can still recall the Victorian era in which cities were growing, bustling and proud places. The Empire was expanding and most people, even the poorest, were confident and purposeful – their doorsteps were polished, and extended families and good neighbours looked after the children, and gave them love and a secure start in life. Great entrepreneurs and politicians from Matthew Boulton to Joseph Chamberlain developed a burning sense of civic pride. They harnessed steam, built sewers, schools and town halls. They shaped events. These were inspiring days of individual progress, enterprise and collective care.

Today, along with the last vestiges of the Empire, the pride and confidence of the industrial era have gone. Now, the younger generation are buffeted by post-industrial events, not in charge of them. Though far more materially affluent, people seem isolated and alone; they are confused by the pace of change. The extended family has shrunk to two parents and a growing number of single parents. The good neighbour is now a scarce commodity. Both street and park have become places where horrific crimes against young children, women and the elderly spread fear beyond the implications of the appalling statistics.

People search for security, guidance and leadership, but they do not get it. Today, the credibility gap between people and the political parties which control local and central government is becoming a cavern. Those resilient growth points which flourish in both neighbourhood and nation do so despite, not because of, any political lead. Democracy depends on understanding and trust between the people and their government, but the understanding has evaporated and the trust has fractured. Democracy is threatened.

The depressing social state of many urban neighbourhoods and the poor quality of political leadership in the Town Hall and Whitehall are each causes of concern. Together, they represent a very serious problem. Matters could get worse, not better, unless clear-headed thinking leads to bold and fresh action. Where might the lead come from and what might the bold action comprise?

The past has gone. However nostalgic we may feel, it is not possible to go back and recreate it, so it is essential to move forward and begin to create new certainties, securities and forms of democracy appropriate to a new age and a new generation. This book has its origins in a conference which was held in Birmingham in November 1994 which was called to grapple with questions posed by two Community Development Trusts, The Settlement in Aston and St Paul's in Balsall Heath, and by Birmingham's Council for Voluntary Service which represents all voluntary organizations in the city.

These three agencies were concerned because an increasing number of people in Birmingham were asking them how neighbourhoods can be made safer and more homely places for the developing child and old folk alike. It seemed to these voluntary organizations that as part of the charitable or third sector they were increasingly being pressed to play a pivotal part in answering these questions in positive, practical ways. Yet at the same time, the potential of voluntary organizations was also being undermined by industrially derived, Lady Bountiful images of them. On the one hand, voluntary organizations were charged with being 'do gooders', peripheral and part-time 'volunteers' who, as such, should be given neither funds nor status. On the other hand, they were being expected to make a vital contribution to the reconstruction of a sense of place, belonging and community which the public sector seemed increasingly powerless to influence.

These Birmingham-based agencies drew the conclusions that the welfare state can no longer answer all the needs of post-industrial society and that 'the community' and its agencies will increasingly be expected to play a key role in resolving problems and opening opportunities. Thus, they asked: What new role should the third sector strive to fulfil? Further, if 'community' is to play a fuller, more robust role, what implications does this have for its traditionally weak and dependent relationship with both the private and public sectors? If 'community' is to become strong, then what adjustment needs to be made to the traditional role of the public sector?

The questions posed by the three local agencies struck a chord with three national ones, the new think-tank DEMOS, Business in the Community, and Common Purpose. Though London based, these three agencies have regional outposts in over one hundred urban areas in the country. They agreed that the questions being posed from Birmingham were also being asked by people in every urban area in the country and, indeed, by a growing number of politicians. The problem identified in Birmingham was not just local, but national. Any solutions should also, therefore, be applicable in neighbourhoods and urban areas in all parts of the country.

This book is not a simple transcript of the resultant conference which the three local and three national agencies sponsored; some contributions have been omitted, others rewritten, and new chapters have been added. The book is, therefore, a development of the debate which took place.

It is in four sections. The first section asks whether people's fears about the poor quality of urban life are justified and whether the sceptical, distrustful attitude of ordinary people to the political parties means that politicians have become part of the problem. Bob Tyrell, Director of The

Henley Centre, Frank Field, perhaps the most respected of all back-bench MPs, and Charles Handy, writer and teacher, show that these problems are real and not imagined.

Indeed, two scenarios beckon us. The one suggests a grasping, individualistic, rapidly changing future in which the gap between those who have 'made it' and those who 'fall by the wayside' widens in divisive ways. The other scenario is less clearly defined, but indicates the need to find more responsible ways of caring for children and finding ways by which all can contribute to a more caring society.

The second section of the book begins the search for remedies to problems and ways of strengthening the second scenario with the help of Amitai Etzioni, the founder of the communitarian movement in the USA. He poses questions and suggests solutions which challenge many popular assumptions and which do not fit into either conventional left- or right-wing political categories. He insists that the basic building blocks for both neighbourhood and community are the values of responsibility and obligation.

It is increasingly clear to those working at the coal face of the third sector that ways of strengthening the family must be found which do not involve going 'back to basics', but move forward to ensure that the developing child is raised in a secure and loving context. Today's concentration on rights has caused many, from the highest in the land to the lowest, to indulge their appetites. People now need to balance their individual rights with a sense of responsibility towards children and each other. Penalties are not proposed, so much as a change of heart. Just as an educational campaign has persuaded many to give up their selfish smoking habits, so a sustained educational campaign is needed to rediscover the common sense of responsibility towards children and each other.

Shorn of the support of the extended family, the small, unconfident, voice of the single- and two-parent family needs to be amplified by schools and also by unions and employers in the workplace who must create the space for the practice of parenting skills. Social security benefits and tax incentives must encourage people to live and stay together, not force them apart. We must again expect the neighbour to be bold enough to take an interest in those who live next door. The video cameras which identified the young children who led James Bulger to his death were not 'snooping'. The many hands which reached out but withdrew before they could protect him need to be given the courage to 'intervene'.

The family and home do not exist in isolation. People need a confident and self-reliant neighbourhood to help them to find the sense of security which can only come through belonging to a community which has shared traditions, ambitions and values. Most neighbourhoods have one or more residents' groups. From very small beginnings just a few years ago, there now exist over a hundred thousand Neighbourhood Watch schemes. Each city can boast of voluntary agencies which employ one or more staff to run an advice bureau, a play or a youth group, a nursery or a community newspaper. They do so against the financial odds and the culture of dependency.

Yet each neighbourhood's residents' group needs the vision and funds to form a Community Development Trust along the lines described by Anita Halliday. Each Trust should be properly funded by a national body with regional branches in every area of the land, as the extract from the Borrie Commission on Social Justice outlines. Chris Wadhams shows the crucial role which housing associations can play in further supporting Development Trusts. The work of Trusts can be complemented by schools, particularly primary schools. As John Rennie explains, many schools are underused community facilities which can join hands with others to form family centres. They can provide rooms and a 'village' hall in which the unconfident can forge a new partnership with the expert teacher, doctor and nurse.

In turn, the professional needs to find new ways of tapping the expertise of the parent and resident who often know best what their child and neighbourhood need. In future, local agencies should be built and managed *with* people not *for* them. New, mutually respecting, partnerships are needed between professionals and their clients/customers. Joe Holyoak explains what is entailed in 'Planning for Real', an exercise which enables an entire neighbourhood to redesign its environment and raise its sights. Indeed, as Carl Chinn, community historian, explains, many of the once outlying villages which became buried beneath the advancing industrial urban sprawl need to be excavated and given a new sense of identity and pride.

Those who staff the Development Trust, community school, housing association and co-ordinate 'Planning for Real' projects and excavate the village-like identity of urban neighbourhoods are the outriders of a new breed of professional. They are the 'social or community entrepreneurs' whom Inger Boyett and Don Finlay of Nottingham University describe. Their task is to stitch together the tattered warp and weft of life in dispirited neighbourhoods, materially poor and affluent alike. Like the Development Trust, these new professionals need to be funded properly. Usha Prashar, who directed the National Council for Voluntary Service, argues that this will lead to much-needed local benefits and to a third sector which is no longer peripheral but central to the modern town and nation.

In showing how vibrant neighbourhoods can be built and sustained, Amitai Etzioni, Anita Halliday, Chris Wadhams, John Rennie, Joe Holyoak, Inger Boyett, Don Finlay, Carl Chinn and Usha Prashar cross the i's and dot the t's of community in very practical ways which should be compulsory reading for every local and national politician. But it is also reasonable to ask: 'Where's the beef?' It is all very well to discuss family, social, housing and educational matters, but the economy and work remain crucial if any solution is to be real and lasting.

The third section of the book starts with Charles Handy's insights about the nature and organization of work in modern society. At the turn of the century, industry required only 20% of the population to be educated. These privileged few then managed a vast semi-literate and semi-numerate manual workforce. At any one time only a tiny percentage of people were unemployed, perhaps 2%. These temporarily unemployed people needed a welfare state for a few weeks before finding new employment.

The nature of work has changed beyond recognition. Charles Handy points out that a job for life for the male breadwinner is fast becoming a thing of the past. The old factory and the production line have gone, and the new workforce is organized into small teams of skilled people who know more about how to do their job than their head office. They have devolved budgets and control, so head office is no longer the sole repository of knowledge. It needs to be small and to respond to suggestions which come from the bottom up. Technological change ensures that specialisms and skills become redundant several times in a lifetime. So, today all need to be highly skilled if they are to keep finding and creating new forms of work and the nation is to compete in the new global economy.

Therefore, we also need a high quality education, not for a mere 20%, but for all, and adult training and retraining which are lifelong. But good education only makes sense when it leads to work. As the modern business 'downsizes' and technological change renders existing skills redundant, more and more people become unemployed for longer and longer periods and at an increasingly impossible cost to the welfare state. The high modern level of unemployment is a scourge which destroys family life, breaks communities, lays waste to neighbourhoods, squanders the nation's sole remaining modern asset – its people – and makes schooling irrelevant. If we are to educate everyone to the best of their ability and create a new sense of endeavour and enterprise then we need a sustained national crusade to create new jobs, if necessary through a range of great public projects designed to recreate a sense of communal, civic and national pride.

Ian Morrison, Director of Birmingham's Council for Voluntary Service, gives a compelling and unexpected exposition of the economic and job-creating power of the third sector. Karin Jacobson, from the DUSCO Corporation, shows how enlightened self-interest can lead the private sector into developing productive new relationships with the third sector. David Grayson details the mutual interest which the three sectors have in each other and calls for a network of 'movers and shakers' which, if plugged into Internet, could act as a vital national and local resource. This section is brilliantly concluded by David Gee, an environmentalist, who demonstrates that care for the environment is no longer a marginal but a vital preoccupation for any neighbourhood, business and city as well as the nation. This third section adds real weight to the soft social plea of the second.

The fourth section accepts that economically viable, robust communities and well-educated people can no longer be accommodated within a dated form of representative democracy which only allows 'ordinary' people to exercise their ability to vote once a year (local) or every five years (central). Once, like factory managers, politicians had a monopoly of information and authority: they could be trusted to represent people in the Town Hall and Whitehall. In today's world of instant information people know as much and more than the politicians. Trust and authority cannot be inherited or taken for granted, they now have to be won and created afresh. New structures are needed which enable people to participate regularly in civic affairs.

As with the rural area which has its parish council, so the urban village now needs a forum through which active citizens can take on a range of neighbourhood functions from the politician and remote bureaucracy. Today, those things which can be done at the level of the family or the neighbour-hood or the town can and should be done at that level. The principle of subsidiarity and self-reliance fosters the quality of responsibility. It creates the sense of ownership and pride and is thus cost-efficient in both financial and political terms.

This means that politicians and the policies of the political parties must change. They are no longer needed to 'tell' people what to 'do' or to 'do' things 'for' them. Rather, the modern role is to enable and facilitate. Today, we need politicians to devolve the role of 'doing and providing' to independent, self-governing, economic and social enterprises which are within the grasp and comprehension of people in neighbourhoods. The non-party political participation of the concerned, responsible, citizen must work in partnership with more responsive representative politicians if the good name of demo-cracy is to evolve with the times and be restored. The challenge to put the structures of participation in place is made by Henry Tam, Assistant Chief Executive of St Edmundsbury Council, and is taken up by Paddy Ashdown, Gordon Brown and Alan Howarth. Along with Frank Field's earlier chapter, their contribution to the debate is remarkable for two reasons.

First, it is not possible to distinguish between their sentiments and proposals. Although they come from differing political backgrounds they sing in harmony from the same hymn book.

Second, they convey a radical and fresh vision of a modern democracy in which previously power-hungry politicians and parties relax their grip on the levers of state and enable the active citizen to play a fuller part in shaping events. They say that they do not mind if this means giving power to people of differing persuasions at the grass roots level as long as it strengthens the democratic process and meets the aspirations of non-political residents.

Theirs is not a dated call for more or less government, for greater or lesser taxation, for collective care or individual rights, for industrially derived attitudes of left or right, but a modern request for a different kind of government and for a new balance between care in the community and individual enterprise, for a new, productive, partnership between the voluntary, private and public sectors.

Through their words and actions, in being prepared to be seen in print and on stage together, these four senior politicians set an inspiring example to others. It is important to build upon the precedent they set.

So, this book aims to further the developing debate which was given focus and impetus at the Birmingham conference. In order to do this, it:

- invites practitioners in the hitherto unsung voluntary or third sector to strengthen their resolve, hone their best selling points and develop a more articulate and self-confident voice;
- introduces third-sector professionals to best practice in the public and private sectors and appeals to these sectors to forge a new partnership of equals with the third sector;
- encourages politicians from all the parties at both local and central levels to follow the lead of Paddy Ashdown, Gordon Brown, Alan Howarth and Frank Field to step out of their dated party political moulds and to search for and boost the common ground.

Already working parties are forming, one which will operate nationally. There are new moves to set up a 'community network' or database of those who attended the conference; this network is being expanded to include people from a variety of agencies. The national community network will also be used to initiate specialist meetings on issues of major importance, to discuss papers and proposals. The network and its offshoots will be operational by the time this book is in the shops. Any reader not yet included in the network should phone COMNET on 0121 449 3808.

The politics of Town Hall and Whitehall have been part of the problem for a dangerously long period. If the pessimistic scenario with which this book starts is to be avoided, then it is time for active citizens in all walks of life to pull the politicians out of their rut and urge them forward. The future of this nation should not depend on habit, happenchance or lottery; we should again take charge of affairs and shape the future. By the dawn of the new millennium community solutions must be put in place so that the nation can celebrate not just fine new buildings, but the ascendance of security and confidence in the neighbourhood, pride in the city, and purpose in the nation.

COMMUNITY –
THE OBSTACLES

*It is important to document and acknowledge
some of the forces which are weakening community
and undermining the political process.*

ME VERSUS US

Bob Tyrell

Introduction

There is a strong argument that our sense of community is under greater threat than ever, that modern life is inexorably eroding our capacity to care about others, even for other members of our own families. Those with a mission to rebuild the fabric of our communities would do well to recognize the strength of these negative forces.

I want to argue that we are poised between two future scenarios: one pessimistic, one optimistic. Which one turns out to be the one we follow will depend in part on the strength of forces which are outside the control of policy-makers and activists at whatever level – national, local or neighbourhood – at which they operate. It is these forces that will be the object of my attention. I will present what I perceive to be the common genesis of both of these possible scenarios, and then turn my attention to the evidence for each.

The common genesis

The need for Britain to develop an 'enterprise culture' seems to be accepted as fact by most shades of political opinion and most commentators on contemporary political culture. The reasons for this are legion. The shift in political ideology in the 1980s is one; the genuine globalization of the world economy is another.

Globalization has become a terrific cliché but it still has some important manifestations, the most telling in the context of the arguments of this chapter being the massive increase in foreign direct investment (FDI). This has changed the nature of the internationalization process.

Until the mid-1980s the dominant internationalizing force was the increase in world trade, which each year increased more rapidly than world output. It made the world feel more 'global' but in a benign, unthreatening kind of way. For example, in the UK our habit of allowing imports to increase more rapidly than exports was a distant sort of problem that resulted in occasional balance of payments crises, devaluations and being told that we could not forever live beyond our means;

but somehow harsh reality never quite hit us. We could keep faith with the Crosslandite view that personal living standards could keep going up with growth but from the increment we could also maintain and improve the welfare state, allow without painful sacrifice those less fortunate than ourselves to benefit from society's increasing affluence and, by the same token, do something beyond rhetoric to sustain a sense of community.

The dramatic increase in the volume of FDI has brought the realities of international competition much more starkly into view. Now, we are all competing on a genuinely world stage to maintain our companies and our countries as a base for international capital investment. If capital feels no allegiance to anything but economic calculation, we have nothing to do but make ourselves economically attractive.

There are many facets to economic beauty, not just low wages and social charges. However, when labour costs in manufacturing in China are 44 US cents per hour against around $17 per hour in the UK, the pressure is bound to be on.

Indexing world output, trade and FDI all at 100 in 1970, by 1993 the output index had reached about 180, the trade index 300 and the FDI index 550. The explosion only started in the mid-1980s and most of the growth has been in FDI to developing countries, particularly China. As late as 1987 FDI into developing countries was running at around $15bn per annum. By 1993 this had grown to over $80bn. No wonder we all feel the pressure is on.

In Europe, Britain more than most other countries seems to have embraced this need for an enterprise culture. This was well expressed in a *Sunday Times* leader on 6 June 1993:

The Prime Minister should state . . . that it is his government's intention to turn Britain into the Hong Kong of Western Europe . . . a low-cost, high productivity, high tech, off-shore island.

More substantively it is evidenced in the reduction in the top marginal rates of income tax in the UK. From having one of the highest in Europe at the end of the 1970s, today it has the lowest. It is also evidenced in our labour market, where the flexibility is illustrated by the fact that we have the largest proportions working both the shortest and the longest hours per week. And, in a Europe-wide survey in 1989 into employers' perceptions of the severity of job protection regulations, the UK was found by a wide margin to have the least severe. On a composite index measure, Italy was top with an index of 120 and the UK was bottom with an index of 50; Germany came in at 90 and France at 85.

The consequences

One of the principal consequences of these developments is a society where the gap between the winners and the losers is growing. There are many ways that this can be illustrated. In Figure 1, below, I illustrate the drastic deterioration that has occurred in the employment prospects of the low skilled. In Figure 2 (page 14) I look at the growth in real income, before housing costs, of each of the groups in the population over the period 1979–1990/91. As you can see, the poorest 5% experienced a 1% decline in their real income whilst the richest 5% enjoyed a 58% increase in their real income.

In comparison with most other European countries, but in common with the USA, this development of a distinct two-nations cleavage was one of the most marked features of Britain during the 1980s. As the 1990s dawned one of its further features was the way that the middle-class 'haves' began to be infected by some of the same sense of insecurity and anxiety as the rest of the population. This is one of the reasons that the recovery from recession has not been accompanied by the return of the feelgood factor. As the corporate fashion for 'downsizing' began to spread to the layers of middle management, so the white knuckle ride of global competition began to be

Figure 1: *Drastic deterioration in employment prospects for the low skilled*

The adult male unemployment rate for the bottom quintile of the labour force (ranked by educational qualifications) divided by the rate for the top quintile

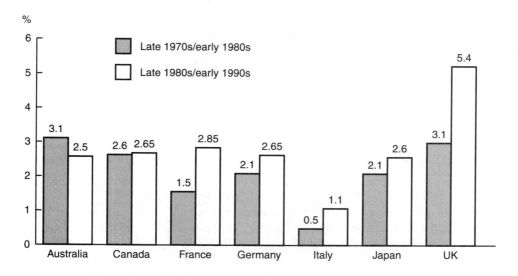

Source: *The OECD Jobs Study (1994)*

Figure 2: *To those who have . . .*

Growth in real income (before housing costs) by vingtile groups,
1979-1990/91

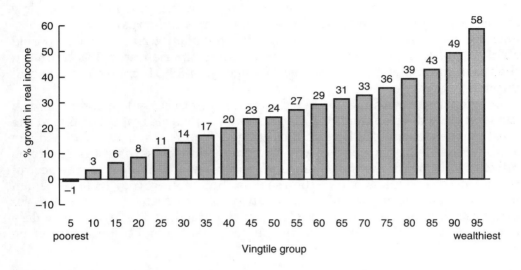

Source: *Winners and Losers, S.P. Jenkins (1994)*

experienced by virtually all sections of the population. No one feels totally safe in their job any more.

So far I have been describing the economic consequences of the forces for change. There is, in addition, another insecurity. As Figure 3 (page 15) illustrates, there has been a dramatic increase in the fears we feel for our physical safety. The question illustrated is from the Henley Centre's regular Planning for Social Change programme. When we first asked the question 'Would you be afraid to open the door to strangers at night?' (in 1981) 35% of the population agreed. By 1993 this had risen to nearly 70%.

Which of the scenarios?

In principle either of at least two future scenarios is intuitively plausible in response to the forces and developments described.

The first is that citizens will say enough is enough. We all know that the old pre-1979 world is like a world of make-believe in the light of the new realities we now face, but the reality we may equally need to recognize is that the costs of the decline in social cohesion and the orientation of citizens and policy-makers towards enterprise and individualism now outweigh the

Figure 3: *'I'm afraid to open the door to strangers at night'*

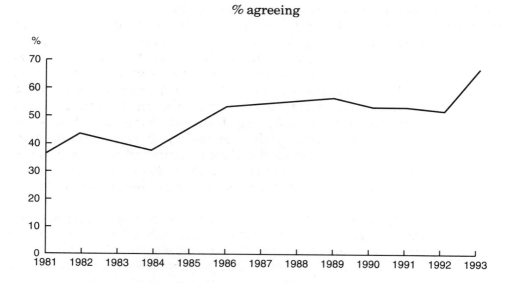

% agreeing

Source: *The Henley Centre, Planning for Social Change Surveys*

benefits. Thus, this scenario might run, we are about to enter a new world of ethics, where the prefix 'public' ceases to be a dirty word and where people reorientate themselves to their community obligations and duties and away from their private concerns. In this scenario you might say that the blitz mentality takes the ascendant as we all muck in together in the face of the new adversities and in the recognition of the rewards of community-spirited activity.

The second scenario could be summed up in the expression 'When the going gets tough those who are most able to be charitable become the least inclined to do so'. This is the scenario of further privatization, in the metaphorical sense of the word, as individuals retreat to their narrowly defined concerns and interests. It envisages a world where individuals feel they have neither the time nor the money to care about others. If one word sums it up it is selfish. Even enlightened self-interest fails to galvanize individuals to community-orientated activity.

The evidence for a world of 'citizens'

There are arguments for this scenario and, by the same token, for optimism about the fertility of the ground on which community-spirited attitudes and action can be built.

The first set of arguments arises from what is known in some quarters as the Ben Elton school of thought. According to this line of reasoning the current individualistic and atomized society is dysfunctional, as it no longer serves even our narrow interests. It was this kind of thinking that might have been behind the hype at the start of this decade about a 'caring nineties' in contrast to the yuppie culture of the 1980s. Although that hype has passed, there is substantive evidence that the sentiment remains alive in different guises. For example, as Figure 4, below, illustrates, during the course of the last decade the answers to our question on the attribution of blame for the problem of high and rising levels of crime have tended to reflect more enlightened attitudes. In particular, it is noticeable how significant the increase has been in the blame attributed to 'less involvement in local community life'. This stood at 25% in 1982 and had risen to 50% by 1993. By contrast, those blaming immigrants decline from 33% to 24%.

Another set of arguments challenges some of the preconceptions that exist about the extent to which local community attachment has been undermined by modern life. For example, the fact is that we are still a geographically rooted society. Although we move fairly frequently we only move short distances. We do not typically move for reasons of work, we move to accommodate changes in family size. Around half the population will move house over the course of the next twelve to fourteen years at current rates of

Figure 4: *The blame for rising crime*

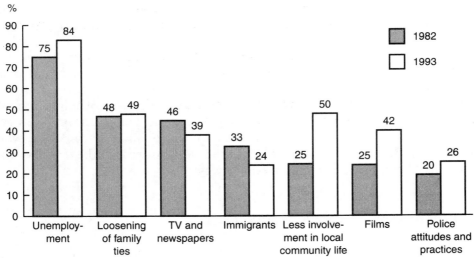

Source: *The Henley Centre, Planning for Social Change Surveys*

mobility, but over two-thirds of these are likely to be less than five miles from their previous address.

When the going gets tough, the tough . . .

Whilst arguments for the existence of fertile ground for a revival of community-orientated attitudes and activity can be mustered, I have to admit to being more impressed by the arguments for the alternative scenario.

To approach the issue head on, Figure 5, below, looks at the results of a series of questions from our Planning for Social Change programme on people's sense of community. The first thing to notice is that these indicators of senses of community vary according to the type of area in which our respondents live. In each case the levels of the indicators are much higher in the rural areas – which obviously bodes ill for more city-based community initiatives.

The second thing is the relatively low levels of these indicators. Even in the rural areas only 35% of the respondents said that they knew their neighbours well, only 29% said that they were proud of the community in which they lived and only 24% said there was a sense of community where they lived. Meanwhile, for those in the conurbations the scores for these questions were, respectively, 28%, 15% and 11%. To state the obvious that

Figure 5:   *A rural attachment*

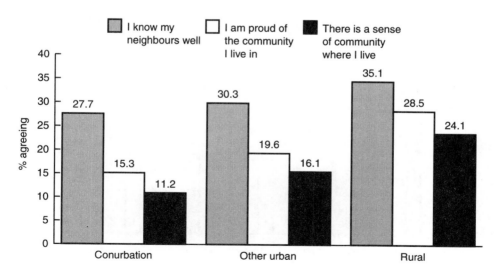

Source: *The Henley Centre, Planning for Social Change 1992*

means that 75% of those living in rural areas and 89% of those living in conurbations say that there is no sense of community where they live!

If we go beyond the way people feel about their communities to the way they relate to civic institutions generally and their participation levels, the picture becomes even bleaker. The decline in and alienation from conventional political participation have been widely rehearsed, and are certainly echoed in our research. For example, those saying that they have 'a great deal' or 'a lot' of confidence in Parliament has declined from 54% in 1983 to 30% in 1993. Similar declines are found in the case of most other institutions, including the church, the press and the legal system; in fact the only ones relatively unscathed by these trends are the armed forces and the police.

Levels of political activism are depressingly low. This is even the case when we look outside the narrow confines of politics to other forms of participation. Figure 6, below, illustrates the point.

A further reason for being negative derives from the evidence of and the inferences we can draw from the actions of the middle classes. Figure 7 (page 19) illustrates the growth in spending on private education over the last ten years. The data is in constant (inflation stripped out) terms. From 1983 to 1988 the levels were pretty constant. Remember, these were supposed to be the feelgood years. Then, just as 'recession' strikes, the figures take off.

Figure 6:   *Crisis of confidence in the British Establishment*

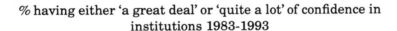

% having either 'a great deal' or 'quite a lot' of confidence in
institutions 1983-1993

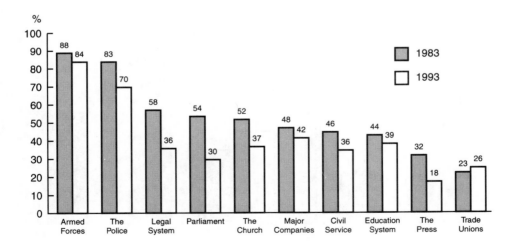

Source: *Gallup*

Figure 7: *The boom in private provision*

Consumer spending on private education at constant 1990 prices

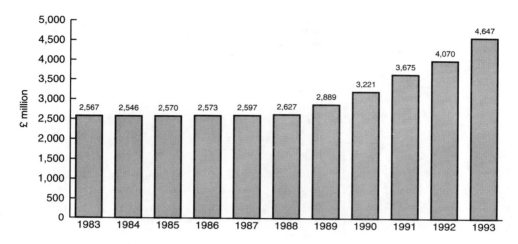

Source: *CSO*

Between 1988 and 1993 there is an increase of 77%.

A number of inferences from this phenomenon are plausible. First, the decline in confidence that accompanied the recession was echoed in a more general decline in confidence in the state (= community?). This would at least be consistent with the failure of the feelgood factor to return whilst the statistics on the economy are generally moving in very positive directions: the spending that is occurring could be described as 'defensive'. Indeed, we have compiled a more comprehensive measure of expenditure which is taking place to replace the services which were traditionally provided by the state. If we add together spending on private pensions, life insurance, private medical care and education, it totals £16bn. In 1994 we estimate it represented 4.3% of consumer spending compared to 3.5% in 1989.

Given that the middle classes appear to have lost their confidence in this more pervasive sense, have opted for 'privatization' against some of their principles and wishes, the question arises: Are they going to feel they have the resources to support the community? Figure 8 (page 20) gives the answer to the financial question.

But, it may be objected, community revitalization does not require money as much as it requires time. Unfortunately the picture on that front provides no more encouragement. We all know about the increase in women in formal employment; indeed, by the year 2000 we reckon that half the labour force will be female. The absence of women from their local communities would not matter so much if there was evidence of men's willingness and ability to

Figure 8: *Declining support for state spending . . . even on universal benefits*

% agreeing strongly

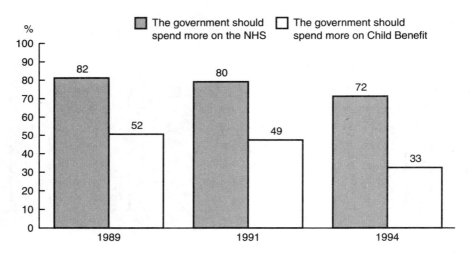

Source: *The Henley Centre, Planning for Social Change 1994/95*

take their place, but that evidence is not easy to come by.

The problem is exacerbated by the additional pressures on women arising from the failure of men to share more equally in the domestic sphere as women's participation in the formal economy has risen. Our research indicates that when all forms of non-discretionary activity are taken into account (including work, travel to work, domestic chores, shopping and child care) the typical full-time female has around thirty-two hours per week of free time, whilst her male counterpart has forty-five hours.

A realistic appraisal of the situation

Those seeking to regenerate the fabric of our community and our society would do well to be realistic about the social reality with which they are dealing. A number of forces, mostly connected in one way or another with technological change and rising affluence, seem inexorably to be driving a pattern of development illustrated in the schematic below.

From needing to operate in 'the community' (public transport, launder-ettes, cinemas, etc.) we have been able to shift our facilities, time and money to the household (cars, washing machines, TVs). We are now in the midst of an individualization of these facilities within the household, a phenomenon which we call the 'cellular household'. It is evidenced in everything from the duplication of ownership of durables (in over 40% of households with children aged 5 to 15 there is a TV in the child's bedroom), the demand for such durables as VCRs and microwave ovens that are so good at allowing household members to do their own thing in their own time, and the duplication of brands: even if it is beneath the dignity of many males to go shopping, it is certainly not beneath their dignity to give their partners a shopping list of their favourite brands. As a result, the for-all-the-household product is now virtually a thing of the past, as family members eat their own brands of breakfast cereals, microwave their own ready-meal recipe dish and wash their hair with their own brands of shampoo.

The cellular household is a powerful symbol of the individualization of social life whilst its expressions encourage, in a very real sense, an intolerance with the idea of compromise and having to 'put up' with collectively provided facilities and services – even when that 'collective' is members of our own family. And, if charity is supposed to begin at home, the cellular household does not augur well for the strength of its legs to carry charity very far outside the home.

2

WORK AND ORGANIZATION

Charles Handy

Bob Tyrell has provided some very telling figures, but he hasn't offered the key one which really scares me. That's one that I came up with about five years ago, half as a joke, half as a warning. Unfortunately, it happens to be true.

'Half by two by three' is the productivity formula for most businesses and now increasingly for most non-businesses, too. Half as many people in three or four years' time will form the core of our businesses. This will be paid twice as well, because we keep the better half, producing three times as much added value. If you say that that's not happening, I have to tell you it is happening in every organization I go into. I went into one organization recently which had 17,500 employees two years ago, but has only 5000 now; and their output has trebled.

Some 44% of the workforce are now self-employed, part-timers, temporaries, or unemployed; very soon it will be a minority occupation to have a full-time job in an organization, and that situation is unlikely to change. America is creating lots of jobs, but they are in the growing 44% and not the other.

There's not going to be any bashing of metal in Birmingham again. And we're not going to be screwing or fitting things together any more; that sort of manufacturing will not be done in our land in the short term. How then do we create wealth? Look, perhaps, at Singapore.

Singapore's ten-year plan says: 'It is our strategy and aim that there should be no physical manufacturing in this island by the end of the century. That is what we want because we can buy everything in. We can buy the hands that bash for they are cheaper somewhere else, of course. We can buy the technology, the money, the design, the marketing, and the selling; anybody can do that. What we can't buy and what we must have are the masterminds who put it all together.'

What counts these days are intelligence, know-how, and practical knowledge; not just facts and the ability to put it together. In a sense, that's terrible, because if you don't have the know-how or the intelligence then you don't have any property in the new society. On the other hand, there's potentially good news, because intelligence or know-how is unrationed: it can go on for ever and ever. Indeed, it's a multiplication sum. It's not like the soil, land or property of other sorts. If I give you my know-how, you get it, but I still have it: that's wonderful. Furthermore, you can make it out of nothing.

Take Bill Gates as an example. Fifteen years ago he was just a chap with large spectacles, a huge forehead, a lot of imagination and a little computer terminal: now he's not just the second richest man in the world. As the Chairman of Boeing said the other day: 'It's outrageous: Microsoft, Bill Gates' firm, is now worth more than Boeing. We could put all their people into one of our parking lots and all their assets into an aeroplane. It's not right, it's not right.' Well, it may not be right but it's what is happening. The good thing about that is that you can do it out of nothing.

We have the potential for solving the alchemist's dream, of creating gold out of nothing, instead of gold out of things and gold out of muscle and the hard sweat of man's brow. That's the good news! Of course, the bad news is that intelligence sticks where intelligence is and know-how sticks with the people who have it, and with the kids that they have, and the schools that they send them to, and so on. You cannot redistribute know-how by act of law as you could with land or with stocks and shares. It's going to be a very difficult process, but the potential is exciting – it's going to change things.

I heard recently that there are seventeen consortia bidding for the new toll roads that the government is asking the private sector to build. Only seven of those seventeen include a construction company. The others are just going to hire it in because that's not what counts: what counts is the ability to put it all together. Anybody can put it together or, rather, anybody with the know-how could make gold out of nothing. That means that this island is not doomed if, in a sense, we do what Singapore does, and we massively invest in the know-how of our people, all our people.

This means that work will take a different shape. The other day two people were talking. One, younger than me, said 'It's a shame, this society, it's a disgrace. There are no jobs for people like me with my experience, my record, no jobs at all, it's a damn shame.' The other person was an electrician fiddling around with the wires that I can't fix. He said: 'I'm so busy: I've got so many jobs on this week, I can't cope.' Two meanings of 'job', you see: one is inherited, a preset role and a place in an organization and customers, contracts; the other one is created.

So, there is lots of work around; but, increasingly it is not going to come in the form of job offers from organizations; it is going to come in the form of customers that you have got to find. So when the government says: 'There will be jobs', they should mean the second sort, not the first sort. We've got to prepare our people for that because we are entering the post-organization society, the age of uncertainty. The result is that half of the people are working all the hours they have and making the money yet with no time to spend it. The other half have all the time but haven't the money to do anything with it. This is resulting in a crazy society.

Therefore, we have to be careful: if there is no education and organization to prop people up, where we are going to get a secure and confident community?

3

POLITICAL AND MORAL

Frank Field

First, I want to look at major landmarks of our political and social environment and then suggest three things that could occur which are relevant to finding effective ways forward.

The first, and perhaps the most important major landmark affecting British society, is the collapse of a moral framework within which we operate. Edmund Leech[1], the Cambridge Don, wrote very movingly about the need for all societies to have a common ideology and that, through time immemorial, ideology has usually, though not exclusively, been a religious one. He also points out that at the time when the moral order, or an agreement on what the moral order should be, breaks down there is massive uncertainty both at the bottom as well as the top of a society. He says that if the general rules which define right and wrong, clean and unclean, cease to have a universal operation in the community, then the community itself feels under threat.

So, one of the things we must do is find the basis for a new moral order. Barbara Wootten, probably the cleverest individual this century, who was an atheist for most of her life but became an agnostic as death approached, said that the first act of faith she had to do as an agnostic was to draw down a set of beliefs by which she could live her life. And just as Barbara had to do that, so we have to do that collectively. The phrase 'moral order' gives us an idea of what I mean.

We now are gathering the fruits of the great change in Victorian society, when biblical scholarship and scientific advance undermined the popular appeal of Christianity. Those people who then became free spirits, who could no longer accept the public ideology, hoped that it would live on and that people would be able to retain the moral values from Christianity without the belief. We now know you cannot, over a long period of time, have an agreement for a moral framework unless there is some acceptance of that dogmatic faith underlying it.

So the challenge we face is to somehow agree a new public ideology or a new public moral order. This is not impossible, given our shared values. The opportunity is still there, but it may not be there in fifteen years hence.

The second landmark concerns the state of politics. It is not an accident that we all hold politics and politicians in such low esteem. There is a danger, however, if we join in the game of knocking the politicians without seeing how politics is related to the collapse of a moral order. Sassoon wrote a footnote to the first poem that he penned in World War I. He commented that if the English were promoted from inferno to paradise, they'd still gather around and talk about the bad old days. There is that very unpleasant side of the English character that wallows in failure and despises success. But we all have a vested interest in the success of our political system.

There are two particular restraints now operating on the ability of this system to deliver more effectively and allow it to enhance its status. One concerns the 'me' society rather than the 'us' society which Bob Tyrell describes. Thus, there is now a feeling of real restraint amongst even radical parties on the limits to which one can propose tax increases to make changes. The other concerns the thought that even if this government is deposed at the next General Election, then the next government's budget, whether it is led by Tony Blair or whether it is a Blair/Ashdown coalition, will be overwhelmingly determined by the commitments the Attlee Government took on in 1945. There is now almost no room for manoeuvre in a budget that can't grow. Thus past commitments, made by politicians long since dead, now determine over five-sixths of the budgets of the next government. So the framework is going to make it very difficult indeed for politicians to pull themselves up by their own bootstraps.

The third landmark acknowledges that we have been living nationally and sometimes locally in an era of a one-party state and of one-party politics. I now see this as I never saw it before when I had to write examination answers. The most important feature in an unwritten constitution is of the fear of losing. The most amazing thing that I witness in politics on the Opposition benches are people in Cabinet, many of whom are very decent people indeed, doing things which appal me. They do them because they are now into a frame of reference in which they believe they can't lose. So, withdrawing from politicians the fear of losing clearly withdraws one of the most crucial restraints of British politics, the fear that you will be 'out' next time and the other group will be 'in'.

The importance of the other side winning next time is not only to reintroduce that fear of losing as the big check on British government, but also because most people haven't noticed that we have entered into a new era of a sustained low inflationary growth. This will be obvious in the next Parliament. Whoever wins the next election is going to be the beneficiary of this new era which, I believe, will be as decisive for politics as the big change in the terms of trade were in the early 1950s. Whoever inherits the next government will inherit it for a long time: that makes it much more important that the radical forces win. Otherwise, the values which we currently see will be reinforced by an economic success which will itself lay the basis for perhaps another fifteen years of power.

The fourth landmark concerns the disengagement from political activity of large numbers of our fellow citizens. Despite the pleasure that we take in being political activists, that's not as widely shared as it was. We see this not just in the lower turnouts for the major elections, particularly in the long term, and compare it with the early post-war period. The trend is down. You could interpret this as Seamore Martin Lipset did; he thought it to be a real sign of a feeling of success and of comfort with the system – it doesn't matter whether people turn out or not. Or you could interpret it, as I now do, as one of disenchantment with the system. It isn't merely about lower turnout, it is for the first time the major issue of non-registration. Since radicals won the battle for the franchise large numbers of people have disappeared from the roll; people generally feel there's little point in putting one's name on the register. So even the turnout figures are not an accurate reflection of the numbers who could actually do so.

The fifth landmark in this arena of the disenfranchisement of political activity is that we are witnessing the collapse of mass parties. There was a brilliant programme on *Newsnight* some months ago where they were doing a study of the Young Conservatives, which in my youth had a membership of 400,000. The membership now I think is about eight thousand. The programme interviewed the chair of the Young Tories who was saying that 'We haven't gone far enough in expelling' people yet. 'We're not down yet to our true supporters and believers, there may have to be further bloodletting.' I say that merely as an example of the collapse of mass parties. But here was one of the largest youth movements in the Western world, now down to a handful of people who are, in true Trotskyite fashion, butchering one another.

The sixth landmark that we have to think about is the disinherited male and the changes in the labour market. These almost suggest that Adam Smith's hidden hand is at work, at long last offering opportunities to women and denying opportunities to men. Particularly singled out for the harshest treatment are males who are semi-skilled and unskilled. If the current status quo continues, those semi-skilled and unskilled males in my constituency will be joined by a growing band of similarly placed individuals who will never officially work throughout the whole of their lives.

Yet, as women become more enhanced and more enfranchised, the labour market is clearly making a distinction between women with great skills and those with lesser skills. The number of full-time jobs has fallen over the past fifteen years. The proportion of women in full-time jobs has increased. This has had a really important impact on our local politics. If one goes back twenty-five years in Birkenhead, well over a third of the councillors were women: they ran all the main committees. But we are now down to just a handful of women councillors. What's happening to women is the reverse of what happened to men in the last century. In radical politics, local government careers were an alternative career for males who were denied the chance of getting on in the world. We now witness women leaving the political arena at a local level and making their own way in the private world of the economy. This has very important repercussions on the health of our democracy: this great, unused, hidden talent, is now being creamed off from local political activity.

The seventh and final landmark concerns the end of free trade. We will not see another American election fought by candidates from major parties who are in favour of free trade. Indeed, we wouldn't need GATT (General Agreement on Tariffs and Trade) if there was free trade. GATT has already ushered in the era of managed trade. I believe we will be moving to a world era of great trading blocs, competing within themselves but very little between them. That is immensely important given that free trade is now clearly in the vested interest of the 'well off' in the community. In the Western world, for the first time, free trade is failing to deliver the benefits it once did to those on the lowest income.

What can be done to tackle these landmarks? Later chapters spell this out, but let me put down three key markers for them. First of all, we ought to try to commit the next radical coalition to agreeing to break up the one-party states at local level. I believe that a change in the voting system is as important for local government as it is for national government. Therefore the great areas in the north, in which Labour have held automatically for generations, ought to be threatened by voters being given as great a choice as is now the case in the grand swathe of seats and authorities in the south, which the Tories held for a hundred years or more but hold no longer.

Secondly, we ought to look at local ways by which we can enhance self-improvement. At the present time, the whole community care budget is used to destroy the natural local pattern of self-support and self-improvement. Much of the welfare state has operated to destroy that most natural and important of human self-help and self-improvement impulses. Let me give you just one example. If we were serious about community care, we would ensure, as each year goes by, that an increasing proportion of the community care budget went as cash to the individuals who need the care rather than directing it through social services. Individuals could then build up their own pattern of care and would thereby naturally strengthen their bond with the local community.

Thirdly, following the experience of what has happened in the Merseyside region via Development Corporations and City Challenge, I hope we will stop using such forms of development in the future. We ought to say both nationally and locally that we are not fit to be trusted with major forms of development at a local level, and that one of the jobs that local authorities should have is to ensure that when areas are up for development then the models we will look for will be the models of Community Trusts and not the statist models that we've adopted in the past.

Of all the negative landmarks I have identified the most important is the disintegration of our moral order. Whereas societies can in the short run live off moral capital inherited from the past, history shows that no society can survive in the longer term unless that moral capital is replaced and replenished. Other landmarks of political concern merely reinforce this problem. If there are to be solutions, they must lie in the arena of breaking up one-party local states and encouraging self-improvement by such means as Community Development Trusts of the kind described in Section 2.

Note

1. Edmund, L., in Peter Pilkington, (1992), *Seek ye First the Gospel*, St Mary's, Bourne St.

COMMUNITY – THE SOCIAL BUILDING BLOCKS

How can community and the wider fabric of society be strengthened?

4

TYPES OF COMMUNITY

Charles Handy

I believe we have to be clear that there are many kinds of community, not just one. First, there is the 'neighbourhood community', the place, the village, the parish.

Second, there is the 'work community', which increasingly is going to be through the super highway, the telephone or other electronic communications system. This is because you do not now need all the people in the same place to get the work done when the work is about information or ideas: it can go through the ether or down telephone lines. Of course, it is very nice to huddle together with people but it's also very expensive.

Offices are totally underused places. Offices are potentially open for 168 hours a week, but most people are only in them for twenty or thirty hours. We will soon discover that office buildings are the most uneconomic assets that we've ever had: people will be pushed out of them. They will be working in British Rail carriages, their cars, their homes, customer's premises and wherever they are, provided they have those little mobile phones and laptop computers with them.

Motorola's corporate strategy says that within fifteen years they want everybody on the earth to have a personal phone, and that when you are born you will get your personal telephone number which will last you for life. It sounds fantastic, but think just what it means: when I call you I don't need to know where you are or who you are with or who you are doing it with. You don't need to be in the office because most of us just go to the office to collect our mail or our telephone calls. That's going to change things. So, the work community can be anywhere. It can be global.

Third, we also need a 'fun community'.

Fourth, we need a 'kinship community', which some people would call a family.

Sometimes these will overlap, but they don't have to. We all need all four kinds of community, but we should not assume that they're all going to be totally complementary; indeed, there is some danger in that. If we say that neighbourhood community has also got to be the kinship community and the work community, then some of our most deprived neighbourhoods will have great difficulty rising out of it.

The 'city' and the 'nation' are fifth and six communities. They are the big 'community of communities'. But I think what is going to be most interesting in the next fifteen to twenty years is that the nation state will wither away and Europe will become a land, a continent, of city states. Cities will compete with cities for pride and culture and excitement and wealth of all sorts. Cities at their best combine all of these things. That's why I think cities are so exciting: they could be the way of the future. Yet if we let the cities die, then these other four forms of communities will be totally isolated, one from the other. Then you would have to get your work from your neighbourhood community and your fun from your kinship community, and that could be very limiting. So we have to be careful and clear about the range of kinds of community which exist and how best to help them to complement and enhance each other, not stifle or become so discordant that they destroy each other.

RESPONSIBILITY

Amitai Etzioni

Consider the problem of the welfare state. It takes various forms in different countries but at the end of the twentieth century it poses some common problems throughout the world. Citizens, by and large, like the idea of a system to assist them if they fall on hard times. But, increasingly, governments everywhere are coming to the realization that the public purse cannot afford to support welfare systems at current levels.

Until now there have been two responses to this. Those of a right-wing disposition say that welfare benefit – in health, education and social security – must be cut, with all public spending, because we can no longer afford it and because it induces a dependency culture and saps individual initiative. Those on the left say that if unemployment was reduced then the national exchequers would have the extra income, from the extra taxes, which would finance existing levels of expenditure. Neither of these approaches offers a sustainable solution.

Nobody is simply a helpless victim. So it is no good the left blaming The System for the fact that the poor are still with us along with all the other social ills. There are hardworking, morally upright people in all socio-economic conditions. Hence, nobody should be exempt from contributing to their own betterment to the best of their ability. This means that some services now provided by the welfare state should and could be undertaken by people on their own.

At the same time, those on the right, who see our social ills merely as signs of personal moral turpitude, must face the fact that there are socio-economic conditions that nobody can control which exact undue human costs.

An individual who loses a job due to technological change should not be forced to bear alone this 'price of progress'; society must continue to share these burdens and some welfare state must exist to provide the mechanism to do that. Attempts to abolish the welfare state completely can never be justified.

As communitarians see it, a strong but scaled-back core of the welfare state therefore should be maintained. Other tasks, currently undertaken by the state, should be turned over to individuals, families and communities.

The philosophical underpinning for this change requires the development of a new sense of both personal and mutual responsibility: but how do we work out which activities should be dealt with at which level of society? By applying the principle of subsidiarity. This says that responsibility for any situation belongs first to those who are nearest to the problem. Only if a solution cannot be found by the individual does responsibility devolve to the family. Only if the family cannot cope, should the local community become involved. Only if the problem is too big for it, should the city or state become involved.

The first responsibility lies with the person at hand. Nobody is exempt. Take the most extreme of examples: suppose that as a result of a car accident a paraplegic is confined to a hospital bed. All he can do is operate a pencil-like stick with his mouth, with great effort, to turn the pages of a book. Should we assign to him a nurse's aide to help turn the pages? The communitarian view is that we should expect the confined person to do what he reasonably can, for reasons of both the dignity that comes with making a contribution to one's well-being and the accompanying reduction of burden on others.

The same holds for drug addicts, the poor, uneducated and handicapped – nobody is exempt from making a contribution. In determining what these contributions should be, judgments must be made. This has not been the philosophy of recent times. In dealing with such groups social workers have tended to 'validate' whatever lifestyle they encounter. They must stop doing this and return to their old role as agents of society, bringing core values to those otherwise out of reach. They ought to be 'judgmental' and articulate advocates of healthy, responsible ways of living.

This has far-reaching consequences. We should hence lay a moral claim on one and all to give up smoking, cease abusing alcohol and drugs and to engage only in safe sex. Levying small charges on those who do not respond to social messages is justified. In the United States some private health insurers charge $12.50 less a month for those who do not smoke, which of course is the same as imposing a $12.50 monthly fine on smokers.

While in general, increases in user fees and co-insurance amount to regressive taxation, small charges on 'sinful' behaviour are a proper and effective way of expressing the values of the society. Significant improvements in lifestyle would save the society the money needed to cover rising health care costs.

The second line of responsibility lies with the family. The tendency of modern society has been to strip duties from the family and deposit them in state-run institutions. Children are placed in childcare centres and the sick and elderly are put into nursing homes. This latter trend is only beginning in Britain but has progressed further in the United States.

This creeping institutionalization of human relationships is a main source of rising welfare costs. At the same time the public's willingness to pay additional taxes to support further expansions of the welfare state has been exhausted. Combined, these produce a dangerous situation in which families become accustomed to not having to attend to their dependent and vulnerable loved ones, and at the same time are unwilling or unable to finance a system to care for them through the public purse.

The solution lies in families reassuming parts of those responsibilities, especially for infants and for those among the sick and elderly who can be maintained at home. Earlier discharge from hospitals following deliveries and most surgeries is a prime example.

The result has three benefits: it reduces public costs, it shores up the family, and it gives the patients care which is, under most circumstances, more personalized and less subject to abuse than public service.

But to make this approach feasible, arrangements must be made to make it easier for families to discharge their duties by broader introduction of flexitime, shared jobs and technological arrangements that enable people to work from home.

Other ways to rely more on families might involve encouraging the development of parent co-operatives, in which fathers and mothers take turns attending to a group of their children or elderly relatives, either completely on their own or by supplementing the staff of state services. New ways must be found to ensure that fathers who walk out on their children contribute to their upbringing.

The third line of responsibility lies within one's community. Neighbourhoods can play a useful role in crime prevention and provide auxiliary assistance to firefighters and emergency personnel. Friends can reduce the need for social work and some forms of mental health services. Civic associations can be a source of loans.

Such notions are not fanciful. Consider the example of Seattle. Some years ago its health authorities were alarmed by the discovery that those experiencing a heart attack had to be admitted to a hospital within four minutes to avoid irreversible brain damage, or worse. The cost of upgrading the city's ambulance service to cover this was prohibitive. Instead 400,000 citizens, nearly half Seattle's population, were trained in first-aid techniques to re-start the heart; the result is that now a volunteer is likely to reach a victim within a minute anywhere, at any time, and at little public cost. The training helped make Seattle a city in which people are each other's saviours; people get to know one another socially in cardiac resuscitation refresher classes and are proud of their communitarian spirit.

Exactly which duties are left to the community and which are to be kept in the hands of the welfare state matters less than that there is a relatively clear understanding of who undertakes which mission.

The fourth level of responsibility lies with society at large. Society has a responsibility to help those least able to help themselves, to share unexpected calamities and to attend to the few services that the community agrees are best discharged via the state. There is no contradiction between demanding that everyone will do their share and realizing that some still will need to be assisted after and as they discharge their duties.

The best way to determine who qualifies for state services is not through means testing, which stigmatizes the recipients and in the long run undercuts public support for the programme, but by treating entitlements as taxable income. In this way all will continue to receive their child allowance, health benefits and so on but the more affluent the person the more will be returned to the public till through taxes.

Creating community service jobs for all those but the mothers of infants and the truly disabled has much to recommend itself from the standpoints of morality, psychology, and the generation of share goods.

Much of what has been outlined requires a new spirit. Whatever politicians might say, the true choice for the future is not between the welfare state and privatization. We should recognize that in the past there were other structures in society which carried part of the social load on their own – communities, families and individuals. It is time to rediscover them and create a new welfare system in which all can honourably and reliably discharge their part.

6

DEVELOPMENT TRUSTS

Anita Halliday

Organizations in several parts of Birmingham provide an excellent illustration of the advantages of Community Development Trusts. There is a growing interest in the Trusts because they can help to meet the urgent need to overcome the multiple problems of under-endowed, disenfranchised and demoralized communities. These are communities which need to experience a surge of regenerative power, capable of carrying them from their position far behind other areas in economic, social and environmental terms, towards parity.

Balsall Heath is just one such community among many in Britain. It has, and has had for many years, a rate of unemployment of 38%. Not surprisingly, there are high rates of poverty and illness, children do not do as well at school as those from more fortunate communities, and young people might grow up without ideals and without much hope. But over the last twenty-five to thirty years, a remarkable host of voluntary organizations has been created in Balsall Heath. In its one-and-a-half square miles, residents' associations, religious associations, housing associations, business associations and self-help groups of many kinds have come into being and worked for the improvement of the area.

Every year, the number of voluntary organizations has grown and the character and quality of the area have changed for the better. It is hard to say how many organizations there are in all; at this time, though, there are fifty or more churches, mosques, chapels, temples and other religious organizations in this urban village. Each of these has within them four or five other voluntary groups. Secular organizations are equally active and numerous, especially now that schools are so closely aligned to voluntary organizations. They also have fostered many other groups – playgroups, parents' groups, latchkey schemes and adult education groups.

It is evident that in the Balsall Heath community almost all residents – of whatever age, sex or cultural background – must be involved with one or other local organization, or perhaps with several. This is extraordinary, for social scientists have taught us to understand that local communities have been dead and buried for decades in our advanced urban society. Yet Balsall Heath has not only many separate voluntary groups whose work is as varied as that of the city council itself, but it has co-ordinating organizations which bring the different groups together to work on matters of common concern.

While housing association members seek to improve housing, and residents' groups have tended to concentrate on environmental matters, other groups have brought nurseries, youth clubs and day centres for elderly people into being. They have also joined together to form a Liaison Committee with the police to consider questions of law and order, and the different groups have combined to form a Practical Care Committee which strives to oversee neighbourhood health, hygiene and safety. A Play Council brings together all groups concerned with children's play. There are other partnerships, including a new partnership of the schools in the area. All partnerships are concerned to share resources of participating groups and develop common approaches to problems for the community as a whole.

A further extension of Balsall Heath's organizational development is the 'Building a Better Balsall Heath Campaign'. This has successfully brought together all the individual groups and constellations of groups to work on an Area Development Plan, through conferences and committees and meetings over the past fifteen years. This has brought the area close to the point where it has built its own Community Development Trust.

Sceptics and cynics have doubted that such a hive of activity can be found in a materially deprived, inner-city area. But they visit Balsall Heath and concede that the evidence is indubitable, for the organizations exist in plain view. It is then felt that 'ordinary' members of the community cannot have done this: there must be some sovereign bee somewhere who is responsible for all this activity. Or maybe a swarm has been captured elsewhere and brought to a carefully constructed hive? For if community is dead, there must be another explanation.

In fact, the activity of Balsall Heath's voluntary groups has been determined by the members themselves. St Paul's Community Project is typical. One major aspect of its work is activities for children and young people in out-of-school time. This part of St Paul's work started in the mid-1960s when the area was full of derelict housing and rubbish tips, with no parks, playgrounds or youth clubs. A lot of anxious parents and many eager children wanted places, ideas and leaders for play. There were local people who had the vision, some time and some experience which helped their will to work for play resources in the area. Now, after a thousand community and committee meetings, hundreds of negotiations with city and government officers, countless jumble sales and other fund-raising events, and after a quarter of a century of play and youth programmes, the part of St Paul's Project which is its 'Venture' has grown from rubble-strewn site to purpose-built Centre. Another part of the Project, adjacent to the Venture, has grown from rabbit hutch to City Farm in the last fifteen years. A pre-school playgroup has grown into a full community nursery school and day-care centre for under-5s.

The same process of gradual, hard-working, painstaking and often painful development is the story of all Balsall Heath's voluntary organizations. For example, Apna Ghar is an organization which runs a Day-Care Centre for elderly people, mainly of Asian origin. They first began to meet ten years ago on benches in the local park. The elderly people who met in the park knew very well what kind of Centre they wanted: one where, above all, their language, religion and culture were understood and respected. They have worked for their vision of care in the community long and hard, and they now have their own battered but cherished premises.

The voluntary organizations of the area are, beyond question, built and managed by members of the community. The schemes of work described are run by committees and sub-committees which have sixty or so people on them. The groups have built and are building, over time, solid foundations for structures that will last, aim high and produce good work. There are no passengers on such committees, nor any reason why there should be: there is little status and there are no perks attached to being part of a voluntary organization committee in Balsall Heath.

The British were described by Napoleon as a nation of small shopkeepers. His implication was that petty, self-serving and unimaginative minds would not do well in competition or in conflict with Europe. Of course, it was Napoleon who failed to check whether the stores were open before setting out in winter for a long stay, with a large party, in Russia. Yet he was not always and entirely wrong. We do seem to be a nation of entrepreneurs. However, more of us are social than commercial entrepreneurs. A lot of the business we initiate and undertake is not for personal or private profit but for community benefit. This is a vital point.

The example of Balsall Heath shows that all kinds of people run all kinds of voluntary organizations. They do so because they know what services and resources are needed in their area and they want to work to secure them. They live in the community and thus have detailed and intimate knowledge of it, have investments in its future and have ties with many of its members whom they want to support. They are careful for their own sake, careful for the sake of others who know them, and careful for the future of their children and their neighbours' children.

Local voluntary organizations are not perfect, but they do have advantages when it comes to accountability: their works are very visible to those who want or are interested in their services. The question, 'Who is responsible?' is easily answered when it is asked of them. The nature of their work is not distant and complex: it is simple and accessible. If their service is not good, if resources are badly managed, if clients are dissatisfied, this is soon transparent to all. Voluntary organizations know that they cannot run a school, a play centre, a nursery, a day-care facility, if no one wants to come to it. For no one has to come – if people are not pleased they will say so.

Even if local people might be deceived into believing that service is good when it is not, voluntary organizations can soon expect to hear from city officers, from government officials and from their bankers if standards are not maintained. If they are in danger of going wrong, everyone will say so.

Local organizations have to start from the bottom, having to earn their support and go on earning it: nothing can ever be taken for granted. Like the private business, the voluntary organization must work its way and keep on working its way to success. People will only support it if they value its work.

The fact that local people value an organization does not mean that they can fund it. People pay national and council taxes. In Balsall Heath the generally unemployed citizens cannot pay additional contributions to voluntary organizations which help to provide the extra regenerative surge they need to catch up with other, luckier areas – people have no money left over to do so. All they can do is express their sense of injustice. They will say that they would have liked to contribute; however, unlike the person of good education, good expectation and good income, they cannot pay to help their child succeed.

If the depressed areas are to come from behind to parity with other communities, they need additional contributions. It is analogous to the situation of the middle-class parent whose child is behind others, and who needs to invest in private education to help her catch up. Voluntary groups must look to city councils and to the government to finance their local services. They must even look to Europe, hoping for a more objective evaluation than Napoleon's was.

It is very difficult to get support for resources. Voluntary groups need finance, particularly for premises and for employees. Both government and local authority may define applications for finance as illegitimate. Archaic, confused and expedient concepts of voluntary organizations are used to devalue their claims:

- 'You are a charity. We may give you a small grant towards your costs to encourage your good works.'
- 'You are filling a temporary gap in our provision. We will grant aid to you as a kind of amateur and emergency facility.'
- 'You are providing, in a specific aspect of your work, a service we require. We will pay for this service but not for your organization.'

The last formula, like the others, is only a way of dismissing the claims of voluntary organizations to be repaid the cost of providing their services. It interprets 'voluntary' as meaning that a substantial part of the work will be provided at no cost. This perverse definition of 'voluntary' ignores its true meaning. In the community, a voluntary group is one which is set up by the free will, free decisions and free spirit of those who set it up and determine its policies. The concept differentiates in a helpful way between voluntary and statutory or local authority organizations.

Even though voluntary organizations need to recover all their costs in order to survive (how can this not be so, if they are to provide useful and valued services?), they are still cheaper than many competitors. This is so because they are not trying to make a profit for private enjoyment. Equally, they are not part of larger bureaucracies which have costs which are increased by the need to employ people to ensure that others are conducting the business properly. Nor are they quangos where, we understand, committee members can only be expected to serve if their public service is underwritten at considerable public expense.

Voluntary organizations give good service at low cost because members wish it to be so. Their activities and expenditure are carefully scrutinized. Those who create them care too much for their work to allow inefficiency or irresponsibility. The organizations have been built to make a positive difference – it is a matter of pride and honour to members that there will be no waste.

Community Development Trusts take the ideals of voluntary organizations and partnerships of voluntary organizations a step further. With public blessing and support, a community can set up such a Trust to plan for the solution of its multiple and overlapping problems, in a coherent and co-ordinated way. Work to solve the problems can be programmed over a period of time. Resources will be focused and little will be wasted on vain or duplicated endeavours. The power which is harnessed – the enormous power of the voluntary will of thousands of citizens – is even more effective for being concentrated in this way. It retains its qualities of vitality, initiative and relevance to community needs. It can power the community to the forefront of prosperity.

7

NEIGHBOURHOOD SCHOOLS

John Rennie

It used to be a commonplace that there was nothing new in education – all apparent novelties were simply re-working of old ideas. The last few years have given the lie to that and teachers are justifiably disgruntled about the sheer weight of change, and the pace of it, even if much of it, still, is old wine in new bottles. This chapter will take the same course for there is surely nothing new in the idea of the primary school as a beacon of activity, meeting the broader needs of its neighbourhood.

Older people in education will remember the excitement at the appearance of the Plowden Report in 1967. Addressing the effects of disadvantage in our society in education, at a time when, unlike now, unemployment and homelessness were, relatively, very minor blemishes on a nation and economy which was broadly stable, the Report brought vividly to life the problems faced by many children. Not the least important outcome were the Educational Priority Areas (EPAs) which produced so much new and even startling thinking in primary education. The most effective and original leader of an EPA programme, as well as being the most influential writer about EPAs, was Eric Midwinter. His seminal books stand as testament to the novel notion of parental involvement in schools, schools' involvement in the community and vice-versa. The Community Development Projects (CDPs) which followed EPAs as the next large-scale government programme focused more on wider issues and only one or two of them included education as a major component. Nevertheless, they did begin to implement some of the EPA values and strategies in different locations.

Community education in its modern manifestation began as very much a schools movement. For whatever reasons – and there were many – the emphasis shifted to secondary level though parental involvement came to be broadly accepted, at least intellectually, as 'a good thing'. However, community education moved on. Now, the best practice is found not simply in the education sector but in the fields of health, economic development, social services, leisure and environment. Since the drive and style of such work are equally applicable to schools, it is worth exploring here the elements in modern community education.

First, it is about lifelong learning. This is much more than mere adult education, vital though that is. It is a practical acceptance of the fact that people have learning needs throughout life – 'from the cradle to the grave' community educators say – which change at different stages for us all.

Second, equally importantly, these needs can be met in a variety of locations and in many disparate ways. It does not have to take place in a school or college. Our African colleagues say 'each one, teach one' – it does not have to be done by trained professionals.

Third, because there is a need to broaden access to reach groups previously ignored or untouched, institutions must open up in terms of their style of community contact and their style of teaching/learning.

Fourth, needs are best met close to where they are seated. A mother of a pre-school child needs provision on the doorstep, not two bus-rides away. Youngsters want to meet with their friends in the neighbourhood they share.

Fifth, the problems in our communities are rarely one-dimensional. Unemployment often leads to crime; homelessness often leads to exploitation; poverty and a stark environment often lead to violence. In any community, there are always different bodies, agencies and individuals addressing those issues, often in isolation and often ignoring other apparently disconnected problems. Community education's solution is inter-agency collaboration – partnerships between the public, private and voluntary sectors focusing on neighbourhoods rather than single issues. The new Single Regeneration Budget (SRB) could be an engine to encourage change in this direction.

It cannot be denied that schools are uniquely suited to provide the base for activity of the nature outlined above. For example:

- School buildings are often the finest public facility in the neighbourhood – sometimes the only one. Certainly they are the most well-equipped, suitable for large numbers of people and, all too often, the only safe building in certain neighbourhoods.
- Schools belong to the people.
- School buildings can be utilized for 14 hours per day, seven days a week, to meet community needs.
- Since the infrastructure is already in place, the cost of additions or conversions to accommodate additional purposes is usually quite reasonable.
- Most schools already have at least a measure of dual use in any case. Typically, there is a ready audience of young people and adults who are coming and going from the building on a regular basis.

These criteria are not met, in any community, by other facilities – not even by a community centre. The sheer economic sense, alone, justifies the case for using schools. Two recent publications from the USA spell out the advantages and practicalities of this notion. *Full Service Schools* (Joyce Dreyfuss)[1] describes schools with additional public service elements such as primary health care provision and argues the case for expanding this concept. The UK experience in places like Abraham Moss Centre in Manchester showed us the pitfalls of divided management responsibilities and the incompatibility of some quite disparate sets of provision. Provided the lessons from those disappointing experiments are taken on board, there is considerable mileage in this notion of a 'one-stop' provision. A booklet produced by the C. S. Mott Foundation of Flint, Michigan, offers some practical examples of such work in action.[2] It is called *Joining Forces: communities and schools working together for a change* and it was inspired as much by the need to find new ways to attack rising crime and increased poverty as it was about educational issues.

The Mott booklet takes the commonsense step, too, of deliberately avoiding the labelling of this kind of activity – which usually only leads to 'turf' problems and management battles. The booklet says: 'So regardless of whether you call it community education, community schools, community collaboration or something else again, or whether today's efforts are simply a new generation's tweaking, what matters is that we nurture any opportunity to bring people into partnership with their community.'

It is not argued here that schools provide a universal answer to the provision of human services: far from it. Developments like the Sutton Centre have shown what is possible when a school is placed right in the commercial hub of a town, and the human service provision is all round it. In big cities other tensions can make multiple use, to some extent, an unnecessary duplication. What is argued here, though, is that all the elements which make schools easily accessible are the reasons which make them desirable and acceptable for other purposes. Most primary schools, except those in rural areas, have a catchment area of about two and a half thousand people – not a bad definition of a community. It is human scale, small enough for people to know each other, large enough to demand a range of service provision.

The Community Primary in action

At a time when the costs of all public services are seen as the taxpayers' burden, in a way which is never applied to defence costs, how can we afford to use prime assets so sparsely? An expensive school building, opening for seven hours (at most) per day, for five days per week, for 40 weeks per year, is a luxury we can no longer countenance. It means that working people who have to pass the school gates to and from work may never see them open. It means, also, that a school is open only for 16% of the total time and accounts for the fact that a child's school life in this country lasts for about 15,000 hours. So, the Community Primary School might be open from 7.30 a.m. to 9.30 p.m. for five days per week and for about twelve hours over the weekend – all for 50 weeks of the year. That virtually trebles the opening hours and suddenly all things are possible.

The day might start at 7.30 a.m. with an 'out-of-school' care club. Encouraged by progressive organizations such as Education Extra and Kids Club Network, this kind of provision is beginning to emerge in many parts of the country. Often, they will provide a light breakfast but always they offer a warm, safe environment in which parents can feel confident in leaving children and which the children themselves can find enjoyable and stimulating. Current funding policies mean that a charge has to be levied but this is usually at a nominal level. The social and even demographic reasons why need for provision such as this has arisen are obvious. So, the need is evident, the facilities are available and costs can be covered. All that is needed is some goodwill and an ability to organize.

During the school day, the presence and contribution of parents to the daily life of the school will distinguish the Community Primary School from the traditional pattern. First and foremost, parents will be welcomed in because they are recognized as the first and most important teacher of the child. A school which turns that recognition into a tangible involvement in the children's schoolwork, along the lines advocated in CEDC's[3] *Parents as Co-Educators* pack, will reap the benefits. The evidence which proves the benefits (on basic skills in particular) of parental involvement, is now overwhelming on both sides of the Atlantic. From *Raising Standards* (CEDC, 1984) and *The Evidence Continues to Grow* (NCCE, USA, 1987) this has been gradually accumulating. Now, a follow-up publication to the latter, called *The Family is Critical to Pupil Achievement* (NCCE, USA, 1994), has dispelled all remaining doubt. Like its predecessor, this book is an annotated bibliography of literally hundreds of programmes which provide concrete evidence of the educational benefits which stem from parental involvement. Presented with such a mass of proof, it is simply unacceptable for schools not to make every effort to bring in parents as partners.

The best schools will, of course, recognize equally that parents have their own needs. Perhaps the most pressing is for pre-school provision for their younger children. 'Rising fives' (those children taken into school at the start of the school year in which they reached the age of 5) was a successful innovation of the late 1970s. Sadly, new funding arrangements have caused this practice to be discontinued in most places. Yet the costs are little more than marginal and the practice could be readily revived with great benefit.

There was a proliferation of school-based provision for parents and children in the 1960s. 'Mother and Toddler' clubs – later 'Parents and Toddlers' – became popular as did Parents' Rooms in schools, various clubs for mums, parent assemblies, morning coffee etc. Many schools have retained a commitment to such activity, despite the loss of flexibility of funding which has made this difficult.

An associated need – one which can be more readily met when a school has pre-school provision – is parental aspiration for their own educational improvement. Involvement in their own children's education has a remarkable effect upon many parents: it seems to awaken in them a recognition that their own education can still advance. A Community Primary will respond to this by brokering some kind of provision for meeting this need. Perhaps the best example is provided in the City of Coventry by the Henley College outreach programme. Here, the local community education staff, having succeeded in involving parents deeply in their children's education in schools and in the classroom, found that groups of parents were beginning to negotiate their own 'curriculum'. They eventually become a 'class', on the books of the local Henley College of Further Education, taught in the Parents' Room of an infants school by a further education lecturer. Style was vital: it was essential to have an informal approach not based on traditional further education methodology. These were, after all, women who had no previous success in education and who would have blanched at the thought of entering a college. The outcomes have been remarkable. From this one class, the programme expanded gradually over the years, attracting men along the way, to become a regular programme in some seventy local primary schools, from which over seven hundred students attain some accreditation each year. Truly a scheme to reach students which other schemes cannot reach!

Adult Basic Education (ABE) has become increasingly successful in recent years owing to the pioneering work of the Adult Literacy and Basic Skills Unit (ALBSU). The confidence which parents begin to feel in becoming involved in schools can often help those with ABE needs to disclose their anxieties, which can then be dealt with sensitively without any stigma. The Parents' Room, at a quiet time, can be an ideal and non-threatening, relatively neutral environment for such work.

Similarly, in those many urban areas with a high proportion of speakers of English as a foreign or second language, the Community Primary School is an ideal base. Again, many schools have taken the logical and practical step of providing for the schoolchildren in one part of the school building whilst the parents learn English in the Parents' Room or elsewhere in the school.

One issue on which parents and teachers are always united – and to which successive governments have paid lip-service – is the provision of nurseries on the same site as the primary schools. This is not to discount the efforts either of statutory Nursery Centres or Family Centres or others in the voluntary sector who make pre-school provision. Nor is it any reason for abandoning informal activity such as the parent and toddler clubs. It does seem, though, that the continuity provided by a school-based nursery has special benefits in terms of relationships and unnecessary changes for children. Community Primary Schools are ideally suited to provide such service.

Where the siting of a nursery requires undue travel for a mother with one or more pre-school children, it might be helpful to adopt a flexible approach. One well-established, imaginative scheme in Coventry has a statutory (joint educational and social services) nursery centre with 100 places. On the register, though, are another 150 children who belong to satellite annexes to the nursery centre, based in a variety of community buildings, staffed by local mothers (trained to nursery assistant level) and backed by two peripatetic trained nursery teachers. This scheme was carefully evaluated and the educational advantages were at least the equal of anything provided solely by professional staff. It is now in its twenty-first year and still going strong.

A recent development in the United States has been 'Cradle Schools' which are essentially the 'Ready-for-School' groups so often provided by Community Primaries. Once a school has opened its doors to parents, it is inevitable that pre-school-age children will need to be catered for. The two, of course, go together. Any sensitive teacher will then quickly recognize the opportunity this presents to involve parents in preparing the child for school – not only socially and emotionally, but educationally too. It seems the Americans have taken a commonsensical old idea and, sensibly, adapted it to make it attractive to parents.

At the end of the school day, a Community Primary might well run an 'out of school care club', matching the one earlier in the day but with a stronger emphasis on recreational activities. Once again, it is the cost-effective use of warm, safe surroundings which makes the notion doubly attractive. In a sense, the idea is a throw-back to the old Play Centres, often used in big cities in the 1940s and 1950s as a kind of junior youth club, run on fairly formal lines. Children of primary age remain intensely 'clubbable' even if their adolescent siblings increasingly are less so.

Yet another community diversion is provided by 'supplementary schools'. Originally these tended to be on Saturday mornings and were often founded by Afro-Caribbean parents anxious that their children's schooling was not recognizing their culture and that the children's achievements were suffering as a consequence. They proved popular with the Afro-Caribbean communities and, later, Asian communities began to adopt the idea, frequently in temples and mosques. This clear manifestation of a commitment to education by different communities deserved to be recognized and supported by local authorities, and in a few enlightened cases it has been. The best recognition, of course, is the acceptance into the mainstream – in funding terms at least – of this kind of community effort.

In Leeds, there is a strong and well-established example (CHALCS) which is linked with Education 2000 in that city. The input from Education 2000 is the provision of an evening class for Afro-Caribbean children which focuses on the use of computers. This is appropriate because the commitment of Education 2000 nationally to the creation of an educative community has made a particularly effective contribution in the technology field. A Community Primary is ideally placed to make skills and technology available in the community on an outreach basis as well as by inviting the community in.

All schools nowadays need to be aware of all the facilities and activities available in the communities in which they are set. Ironically, the apparent competitive climate created by the new funding mechanisms has made more schools realize this. Of course, the best schools will wish to be thinking on these lines for better motives and will wish to go much further than merely being aware of what is going on around them. The community education approach adopts 'inter-agency collaboration' as an essential element in its programmes. Since community educators believe that communities have a key role in meeting their own needs – and using all the human and physical resources available in the community to do so – it is a natural part of the work of any Community Primary.

Traditionally, community education began with a 'needs analysis' – a direct survey of what people in the community needed, or wanted or aspired to. Now, to this must be added a community audit – a structured survey of what is available in the community which can help the school best meet its targets and which the school can help in return. The audit will find, at least in urban areas, a range of other bodies with whom they can forge mutually beneficial links. These will include voluntary organizations, Community Development Trusts, businesses, churches, the typical range which can be found in most communities. However, the audits throw up surprising findings. One such, in a very small town in Oxfordshire, threw up no fewer than 160 organizations, including a deep-sea diving club! Of course, only a proportion of these would be in the catchment area of any given primary school, but it is an indication of the strength and diversity of community life which too often lie untapped by the education service.

Implications

What is advocated here is for all primary schools to become community schools. Clearly, not all of them will be able to offer the full range of what is possible. However, all of them will be able to offer some, and many will be able to offer all. It cannot be denied, though, that there are implications to be considered.

First, inevitably, will be the cost. Experience suggests that this need not be as forbidding as might at first appear likely. Very little additional space is required. Coventry provided all new schools with a Parents' Room simply by using the traditional medical room and by imaginative use of the central administration space. Most rooms become dual-use. Although some adult furniture becomes necessary, little additional equipment is required. Many of the activities are self-supporting, even if they require a bit of friendly help from the occasional jumble sale and the like.

Second, staffing is also an important issue. No additional full-time staff are necessary, though a teacher who can be released half-time is very helpful. Finance is needed for bought-in part-time support, although the out-of-school care fees and other nominal charges can largely offset them. Perhaps a greater issue regarding staffing is the in-service training which will be necessary. By and large, teachers have received little or no initial training to help them cope with community involvement. Although not all teachers in a given school will be involved in this way – even in a community school – they will all need some awareness-building. They need to understand the reasons behind new kinds of work since their sense of ownership will then support the work. Current in-service funding might be inadequate to provide the necessary training and it would then need decisions from a higher level than the school itself.

Third, the school will need support. This is linked inevitably to the other two issues but, in addition, there remains a role for the local authority or whichever co-ordinating body replaces LEAs, as now seems likely. It will, of course, be simpler if other local schools are undertaking the same development. Again, this raises the issue of competition versus co-operation and this is addressed in the last section of this chapter.

How will we recognize the Community Primary?

Schools tend to look alike. The teachers and the parents, more than the children, are likely to notice the differences from other schools. It should be possible, though, for a school to ask itself a range of questions to which a high percentage of positive responses would indicate that a school was truly a community school, designated or not. The same questions are equally relevant for outsiders and would include the following:

- Does the school look welcoming and does it signpost clearly the entrances, exits and different sections?
- Is it community-friendly?
- Is there a community dimension to the school's delivery of the national curriculum?
- Is there a Parents' Room?
- Is there a range of activity groups for parents?
- Do parents run their own initiatives in the school?
- Do parents participate in the classroom?
- Does the school help parents to help their children in educational matters at home?
- Is there a parents' newsletter?
- Does the school have a regular scheduled meeting with other agencies in the community?
- Do other community agencies participate in school activities?
- Does the school have an outreach programme?
- Does the school co-operate with other community agencies in specific activity in the community?
- Is there pre-school provision (nursery) on site?

- Is there informal pre-school provision on site?
- Is there a morning out-of-school care club?
- Is there a twilight out-of-school care club?
- Is the school used during the evenings?
- Is the school used during weekends?
- Do staff and parents share in events?
- Does the school co-operate on specific issues with other neighbouring schools?
- Have the staff undergone in-service training in community involvement?
- Does the school use volunteers on a regular, structured basis?
- Is there a teacher with designated responsibilities?
- Does the school have a community mission statement?
- Are all staff committed to this involvement?
- Does the head have this written into his/her job description?

All of these questions will need to be broken down into more specific questions if any real attempt is made at monitoring and assessment. Again, many other questions are relevant – those above are simply a guide.

It will take a considerable time for any school, starting from scratch, to become a community school of the kind which could meet the above criteria. Nevertheless, the first and most essential step is for the school to make a commitment to the ideal. Happily, this is now much easier than it once was. Schools can self-designate as Community Primary Schools, provided the governors agree. Help is available from CEDC for all the next steps.

The schools and the LEAs

Since the mid-1980s, it has seemed as if a war has been waged against local authorities by the government. It has been a war of attrition where the main features have been:

- a steady but by now dramatic decline in the percentage of funding available coming from central government;
- a severe tightening of constraints upon local authority responsibilities, particularly spending (e.g. capping);
- an encouragement of schools to opt out from LEAs;
- formula-funding for schools, cutting the LEA's role;
- steep decline in numbers and functions of LEA inspectors and advisers;
- devolved funding from LEAs to schools.

By the mid-1990s, the LEAs have become emasculated shadows of their former selves. Clearly, there was a need for reform but several babies have been thrown out with the bathwater. The great disadvantage of LEAs was that, like central government, they were bureaucratic and seen as too distant by schools. This has now gone but so have the economies of scale which they brought in providing such services as planning and central purchasing as well as their relatively subjective quality control. Where the grant maintained schools have been established, there, too, the picture is mixed: these schools have the great advantage of decisions being made directly at the point of need. Also, they have the incentive to save money in one area to use it in another. Their disadvantages are that they provide competition of an unhelpful and wasteful kind – unlike competing super-markets, for example. Also, they have failed to deliver on choice – their great raison d'être.

We are perhaps ready now to take another radical but logical step. Simply stated, it is to put the LEAs out of their misery by closing them down and by giving all schools not grant maintained but self-governing status. It would then, of course, be necessary to re-invent the LEAs in another format, with highly specific new roles (not the hazy left-overs which is their lot, now), since they have functions which cannot be carried out by individual schools. At the same time, the LEAs' replacement might become more directly accountable with elected representatives from different sectors.

One model to adopt would be a Local Schools Council of Management, with membership elected from slates of candidates provided by: political parties (proportionate to the local elected Council); churches and other religious bodies (proportionate to the local population); voluntary organiza-tions; businesses, commerce and trade unions; professional bodies; commun-ity groups.

Such Councils would have an executive role as well as a political role and this would include: planning, sites and buildings (as now); central purchas-ing (offered to schools on a market basis); educational psychology, welfare and specialist (e.g. visually impaired) services; quality control (against Council-agreed criteria); innovation (within Council-agreed parameters).

The truly radical element would come from a breakdown of the current LEA areas into more manageable administrative areas. No former constitu-ent area of the old ILEA, now LEAs in their own right, would wish to return to the old structure, despite its many glories. Similarly, a new local Schools Council might break into three or four administrative areas – cities such as Birmingham, Manchester and Leeds have obvious divisions. Each of these would have a Local Schools Board which would, under the Council, super-vise each area on a neighbourhood basis of clusters of ten to fifteen schools. This layer would not be 'heavy' but would be there as an enabler and support to the clusters.

The advantages of this system are:

- decision-making completely devolved to schools on a day-to-day basis;
- cost-effectiveness through shared resources and central purchasing;
- losing wasteful competition;

- building local identification;
- providing local support directly and from nearby;
- retaining innovative leadership;
- increasing accountability;
- providing a broader and more inclusive democratic base;
- removing narrow political prejudice.

It can be argued that this is a community approach (the Local Schools Council is essentially a Community Schools Council but is an LSC because it will be more readily generally understood). All of it – schools and the Local Schools Council alike – would be more effective if central government could accept LSCs as partners in education and not as enemies.

Notes and references

1. Dryfuss, J.G. (1994) *Full Service Schools*. New York: Jossey Bass.
2. *Joining Forces: Communities and Schools Working Together for a Change* (1994). Michigan: C.S. Mott Foundation.

8

HOUSING

Chris Wadhams

The neglect of neighbourhood

Almost thirty years ago, groups of people with a social conscience began to act in a rather strange way. Energized by *Cathy Come Home*, a television programme which graphically illustrated the housing problems faced by vulnerable families, they met in church halls, community centres or in their own front rooms and planned to take direct action to improve the housing conditions of homeless people. They were going to do this not by picketing their council housing departments or petitioning their MP, but by setting up housing organizations of their own.

Concerned by the failure of both the private sector and the state to provide decent homes in secure neighbourhoods, these pioneering volunteers sought to create smaller local organizations, working mainly in poorer areas, to be run by local people to meet local needs. They faced an uphill struggle, for their efforts took place during a time of decline for neighbourhood solidarity which has continued to the present day.

Neighbourhood has, for over thirty years, been a neglected piece of the urban regeneration jigsaw. Despite the foundation of these modern housing associations, in the excitement of the 1960s with the emerging freedoms of a new society, neighbourhood, with its overtones of the blitz, post-war austerity and the complacent 1950s, was mainly a concept to forget. From the 1960s to the early 1980s, organizing round the home generally took second place to organizing round the workplace.

Despite these trends, community action, triggered by protests against clearance schemes in more popular low-income neighbourhoods, slowly began to develop some strength. It was then overwhelmed by the surge of political support for extending the rights of individuals. The dogma that there was no such thing as society and the only way to make a home was to own it, dominated political debate. Only recently has there been any serious attempt to re-evaluate and extend the concepts of neighbourhood and, within neighbourhood, the potential of community action.

The neglect of neighbourhood was acceptable to the Conservatives and, despite some experiments in decentralization by London local authorities, broadly ignored by Labour. That the Liberals and subsequently the Liberal

Democrats, espoused 'community politics', made this neglect even more tolerable.

'On yer bike' was one response to the plight of the increasing numbers of the unemployed. National policy needed mobility, not neighbourhood. The central government agenda in the 1980s emphasizing flexibility, fixed-term contracts and a search for work was in conflict with people's need to recognize kinship, to set down roots, to feel secure. These needs had been under strain for some time; old communities were fracturing and new patterns of life emerging, but the 1980s put the boot into neighbourhoods more firmly.

Many of the potential defenders of neighbourhood were silent, too. For some in Town Halls, including Labour Town Halls, neighbourhood meant activist, and activist meant trouble. Activists were unaccountable and unrepresentative, local politicians demanded 'If you want to get consulted, get elected.' Community action was an irrelevance, opposition to central government was firstly best mobilized through trade unions and latterly by elected local government. Throughout the last thirty years, people of all parties and of none have struggled to maintain the validity of ideas of neighbourhood and community. From defenders of the positive aspects of village life to the many 'ordinary heroes' in inner cities, the idea that individual rights are best exercised and defended in a context of collective responsibility has been kept alive.

From 'small is beautiful' to the recognition that local and global economic issues are intertwined, the theme of development and action on a human scale has never been entirely extinguished. Now in the 1990s when the baleful effects of a dependence on the market alone or on the state alone are increasingly apparent, the need for neighbourhood solidarity is becoming more widely recognized. And the modern housing associations, set up by the volunteers in the 1960s, have a crucial part to play.

The end of the housing honeymoon

Housing has a special place in reflecting national morale. After 1919 it was homes that the returning heroes were promised. In the 1960s demolition and rebuilding were seen as the means of transforming poorer areas. The optimistic view was that the surge of new developments for rent would bring about an end of slum housing and that a new neighbourhood spirit would develop amongst the people rehoused in better conditions.

The optimism faded. Tower blocks and large estates built without social facilities undermined the confidence in council housing, even though less than 10% of our housing stock is high-rise and large estates are the exception rather than the rule. But as influential as these physical problems was the management failure which created petty bureaucracies, inefficient direct labour organizations, poor levels of service and a growing animosity between those who lived in council houses and those who didn't, but who were responsible for managing them.

The end of the housing honeymoon marked a profound change, signalling a loss of confidence in municipal solutions to the problem of tackling housing need. It made it easier for the Conservative Government to present renting not as a respectable form of tenure but as a second-class system for those too poor to buy. The result is that council housing, rightly criticized in the 1960s and 1970s as being allocated as a reward for good behaviour by officials who inspected the bed linen of slum dwellers to ensure tenancies went to the 'deserving poor', is now equally criticized for becoming the housing safety net for the 'undeserving poor'.

Ironically, this loss of confidence had, for a short time, some beneficial effects. It helped create the positive climate for the development of the locally based housing associations. It equally created a determination to tackle the council estates, both by improving the physical conditions but, more crucially, by involving tenants directly in the process of management.

New developments were on traditional lines, low-rise with pitched roofs. Housing associations developed expertise in repairing older houses in inner-city terraces. A few enlightened local authorities, like Birmingham, provided free programmes of re-roofing and external improvements to low-income owners. But this respite was short-lived: the government was determined to tighten controls over local government and brought in capital programme restrictions which effectively ended any new building by councils.

In parallel, a vigorous programme of promoting home ownership and selling off the better council houses led to a polarization, both of the stock and the tenants. The end of the housing honeymoon meant that council housing was firmly established not as a social asset, but as a welfare safety net. Second-class housing and second-class services were deemed to be adequate for second-class people.

Dancing to the piper's tune

The housing associations, set up by the pioneering volunteers, had originally been intended to support the work of local authority housing departments. Their committees intended them to provide an element of choice, to refurbish existing houses and invest in hard-pressed neighbourhoods, to concentrate on special needs; but they gradually took on a new role. New council house building programmes withered, as borrowing to build was increasingly restricted and housing associations began to be spoken of as firstly the main, and finally the sole, provider of new housing to rent. This was not a role housing associations sought and not one they all whole-heartedly welcomed. The associations were well aware that the government's ambition of their simply supplanting the local authorities was unrealistic. Their efforts to fill the gap created by the reduction of council building have been valuable and extended housing choice but the shortfall of homes to rent has grown substantially. Equally, the programme was financially unsound. The assets of council housing were sufficiently mature to allow new building and repair to be financed by borrowing; but since the government held that no risk was borne by the lenders, the government itself being the ultimate guarantor against default, all borrowing was counted within the public sector borrowing requirement.

Housing associations, in contrast, had fewer assets. To enable them to build houses which people could afford to rent, much of the capital cost had to be immediately written off, as a non-recoverable grant. But in government accounting terms, the expenditure, whether financed by borrowing from the Public Works Loan Board or by grant, which itself was originally borrowed by government, was the same.

The rules were changed in 1988. By then, housing associations had created sufficiently large asset bases to allow more of their capital programmes to be financed by loan rather than by grant. Government legislation created a fixed grant regime, thus effectively transferring development risk to the association. Association's loans could thus be re-classified as private and they could now be presented as a cheaper option than council building, since only the reduced grant scored against the Public Sector Borrowing Requirement in year one.

Arcane public accounting rules decreed that giving housing associations 50p towards building a house was cheaper than letting councils borrow and repay £1. With these financial advantages and all-party political support, some of the associations set up in the 1960s rapidly outgrew their neighbourhood origins. The freezing of council building and the promotion of housing associations as the sole providers of new stock are now creating some unwelcome housing outcomes.

The 1988 reforms were conceived as part of the government's private market strategy. Before 1988 both the Department of the Environment and its quango, the Housing Corporation, supervised the work of associations. After 1988 a purchaser/provider relationship was created, whereby the Department contracted with the Corporation to expend a fixed sum of money and the Corporation, in turn, contracted with its clients, the housing associations, to deliver the maximum amount of houses possible for this sum.

Only at the next level, between housing association and tenant, was there no effective internal market, since demand for the product so greatly outstripped supply, that customer choice was a hollow myth. Since competition drove the market, housing associations quite reasonably sought to provide their product more cheaply in terms of the grant they needed.

Thus, a few of the largest associations reduced their neighbourhood renewal targets and the development of smaller infill sites in favour of larger new-build estates, purchased directly from the volume builder. Local authorities, desperate to meet their legal commitments to the homeless, offered land free or at substantial discounts in return for the right to nominate homeless families to the housing created. With cheap land, lower standards and higher rents, housing associations proclaimed their virtue in providing housing for lower and lower rates of grant.

To sharpen competition still further, government action to force rents upwards provided some associations with the opportunity to subsidize development from growing financial reserves. Whilst reserves were essential for reinvestment, their use to reduce the level of required grant for new schemes led to an unprincipled scramble for advantage between associations.

Social rented housing has therefore become an Alice in Wonderland system, where government definition of public borrowing sidelines potentially the most economical public provider whilst rewarding the most expensive. Some housing associations find that by reducing their investment in low-income neighbourhoods to build larger estates and by accepting 100% local authority nominations, they are now housing substantial numbers of very poor families. In the neighbourhoods they are deserting, housing association rents have been forced up by government for the existing tenants and the profits created recycled into these large new developments which risk becoming the ghettos of the future.

Rebuilding neighbourhoods: rebuilding hope

It is time to draw the threads of the neighbourhood development argument together.

As Bob Tyrell has shown, there is no doubt that some of our neighbourhoods are becoming poorer relative to others. There is no doubt, too, that the housing situation of poorer families has worsened in the last decade. But success in the effort to turn the situation in our low-income neighbours round by supporting local economic development has been patchy at best.

Lemann,[1] looking at the American experience, argues that this failure arises from the dislocation of the local economic and social housing agendas. Until recently in the UK, as in the USA, resources have been applied to attempts to regenerate local economies in isolation from other programmes, resources which might have been better applied to other primary targets – improving schools, combating crime or improving housing conditions.

The real successes of the American Community Development Corporations have not been in the high profile, much-publicized local economic strategies favoured by politicians and by many voters, but in the unfashionable, unrecorded and almost surreptitious provision of social housing. Social housing, claims Lemann, is the 'spiritual centre of anti-poverty work'.

Success in the search for a local mechanism to connect economic development, the provision of social housing and broader programmes of neighbourhood development, is a critical policy imperative for the 1990s. And, almost by chance, we have over the past twenty years created a powerful network of honest, well-funded organizations, many with their origins in supporting low-income neighbourhoods, backed by a national regulatory and advisory framework.

The problem is that many of the members of the housing association movement are nervous about broadening their definition of a 'social landlord'. They are wedded to an almost unshakeable belief that only by continuing an expensive development programme for meeting general housing needs can they demonstrate their virility and alleviate homelessness. Yet the supremacy of the housing associations is due only to government dogma in seeking to reduce the powers of local government and accounting conventions which treat borrowing in a different way if undertaken by a housing association rather than a local authority.

The gradual, perhaps reluctant, acceptance of their overall strategic role by local authority housing departments, and the positive impact of the requirement to discuss and identify acceptable levels of service for tenants brought about by compulsory competitive tendering, have created conditions where local authority housing departments may now be ready to bid to resume their development functions.

This readiness will need to be accompanied by changes in the accounting convention for public borrowing, in order to enable housing departments to borrow from the market in the same way as housing associations. The prospect of housing departments again building in partnership with local communities may require new structures, perhaps the semi-independent housing companies now being assessed in a number of pilot studies, or by ring-fencing housing capital, as well as revenue, accounts. These changes will be controversial; but the new vision of locally accountable council housing, together with the cuts in Housing Corporation programmes, may encourage the possibility of a new mission for some existing housing associations.

What better mission could there be for these innovative associations than returning to their roots and becoming the neighbourhood regeneration agencies we so badly need? These associations could limit their development work to relevant special needs provision and strategic rehabilitation of existing housing, including the older properties already in their ownership. They could then devote energy and skills to a wide range of neighbourhood development programmes and partnerships. Appropriate grant support would be available for these housing and neighbourhood regeneration programmes.

Re-targeting the development programmes of key housing associations and returning the main responsibility for the provision of social housing to the reformed local authority sector have three major advantages.

First, it creates the potential for housing association revenue surpluses to be devoted to broader programmes of neighbourhood regeneration.

Second, it provides the housing association 'agencies' with a greater degree of independence.

Third, it assists in accountable governance by moving the responsibilities of their voluntary committees or boards away from treasury management, risk assessment and the financial markets towards housing management and neighbourhood renewal, issues which critically need the skills and knowledge of local people. This 're-balancing' would enable the housing-based Neighbourhood Development Agencies to experiment more whole-heartedly with structures which centrally involve existing tenants as partners in the management process.

Such reforms would not be easy to achieve. They would require the Housing Corporation to be reorganized and its role widened into a National Neighbourhood Regeneration Agency, funding not a Housing Association Grant (HAG) but a Neighbourhood Regeneration Grant (NRG).

The new Neighbourhood Regeneration Agencies would be underpinned by the existing revenue surpluses created by housing associations. In 1992 and 1993 North British Housing Association, the largest association measured by homes in management, collected over £43m in rent and spent less than £14m on staff. Commendably, much of their final surplus was reinvested directly into improvements to the housing stock. But, retained annual revenue surpluses arising from the activities of other housing associations exceed £200m. Creating the capacity of the reformed local authority sector to borrow from the private market, outside the PSBR, would allow new investment to take place which would release the housing associations' surpluses to catalyze neighbourhood renewal work.

Those associations with a national presence or with sufficient stock in a region could become housing companies similar to any local companies created by reorganizing council housing. These housing bodies plus any set up by the private sector could remain providers of general social housing and of special needs housing, where appropriate.

The new accounting conventions would need to address the private sector's claim to need adequate security in advancing loans for development to this new housing sector. But current practice classifies investment in housing, which does create a specific revenue stream, in the same way as investment in health, education and training, where the gains are more generalized.

If the defenders of the status quo claim that even public projects can go bust, it is still illogical to class that risk as 100% certain, rather than take the sensible view that only the notional cost of the risk premium to insure against that eventuality need be measured as public spending.

Could local authorities be persuaded of the value of such semi-independent agencies? For the role of such bodies is controversial. To some

politicians they represent a threat; these people argue that local representative democracy is the best legitimate channel through which people should
articulate their aspirations and devote their energies. Whilst recognizing
that local people may wish to take direct action on specific issues, organized
neighbourhood groups or community action programmes are, from their
perspective, often dominated by a few unaccountable, unelected, activists
who use them to further their own ambitions and their own careers. To
others, such local NGOs are seen as no better than the larger quangos in the
health service and in training and employment, bodies set up to bring in the
private sector, with managing boards selected from government supporters.

Since they may develop at different speeds, the activities of these agencies
can be seen to lead to diversity of outcomes and threaten principles of
equality. Traditionally, the public sector has defined and defended the values
of equality and justice and tried to ensure a fair distribution of resources
across the country. But, too often, the state at both central and local level has
demonstrated its insensitivity and people no longer trust it to deliver.

Others argue that a cultural change in local government is required, to
enable it to engage creatively with local community interests. This task is
seen as of parallel importance to the cultural change in the 1980s which
created the conditions for partnerships with the private sector.

The fear of local agencies stimulating and supporting local action arises
from a confusion between the role of the strategist and that of the activist. In
real life, people wish to be both. So if those whose legitimacy arises from
election concentrate mainly on agreeing an overall strategic direction and
enter into compacts with organizations whose legitimacy derives from
street-level action, progress can be made.

Politicians have most frequently seen their role as representing the
individual citizen. But in some instances, a proxy 'corporate citizen' in the
form of a neighbourhood agency can enable local people to avoid dependency
and to take more control over aspects of development in their own neighbourhoods.

In pure housing terms, redirecting the method of provision also carries a
risk. Perhaps the reform of local authority housing departments will prove
to be only superficial. Once their powers to build are restored, will local
authorities resist further reorganization, reject the creation of housing
companies or locally responsive management systems and revert to a
centrally directed, bureaucratic and welfarist form of provision? Even if it
were set up, would any new local authority-based housing company be
sufficiently entrepreneurial? Housing associations, it could be argued, have
had a five-year learning curve in handling private funding and responding to
the demands of lenders for new financial skills and techniques, and have
found the going tough.

Even if municipal triumphalism or financial naiveté can be avoided, would
the locally based associations buy into their new role? The signs are not
encouraging. An important study assessing the capacity of UK housing

associations to develop into the equivalent of the US Community Development Corporations concluded that they would need to improve their capacity to involve local people proactively in broader programmes of local economic development if they were to grasp the opportunity their far greater housing assets created. A recent survey of housing association voluntary committee members found that accountability to local communities was rated lower than accountability to existing tenants, the Housing Corporation, the local authority and private lenders.

Yet, despite their current reluctance, some of the medium-sized associations might soon be prepared to expand their neighbourhood activities as their bi-partisan political support erodes, their development programmes are cut and their asset cover for private loans becomes exhausted. It is to be hoped that enough of them can be persuaded to view these changed circumstances not as a threat to their existence but as an opportunity to take the lead in rebuilding our low-income neighbourhoods and providing new resources to hard-pressed communities.

The process whereby local people build local organizations and create local coalitions is described by Sivanandan[2] as creating 'communities of resistance'. By waking the sleeping giant of neighbourhood, by bringing more housing programmes, assets and resources under direct local control, these 'communities of resistance' could begin their long journey of transformation into 'communities of hope'.

Notes and references

1. Lenmann, N. (1994) *The Myth of Community Development*. New York Times.
2. Sivanandan, A. (1990) *Communities of Resistance: Writings on Black Struggles:* Verso.

9

URBAN VILLAGES AND NEIGHBOURHOODS

Carl Chinn

In the early nineteenth century, British society was youthful and dynamic. The majority of its people were under 21, and many of them were moving from the countryside to the exploding industrial towns and cities. These were exciting places: they were noisy from the hustle and bustle of masses of people; they were loud from the making of things; they were raucous and raw; they drew in the young, the hopeful, and the work-seekers. Charles Dickens captured their atmosphere in 1837 when he described Birmingham in *The Posthumous Papers of Mr Pickwick*:

As they rattled through the narrow thoroughfares leading to the heart of the turmoil, the sights and sounds of earnest occupation struck more forcibly on the senses. The streets were thronged with working people. The hum of labour resounded from every house; lights gleamed from the long casement windows in the attic stories, and the whirl of wheels and noise of machinery shook the trembling walls. The fires, whose lurid sullen light had been visible for miles, blazed fiercely up in the great works and factories of the town. The din of hammers, the rushing of steam, and the dead heavy clanking of engines was the harsh music which arose from every quarter.

But the great towns and cities were magnets which repelled as much as they attracted. Traditionalists looked on aghast as urbanization transformed the face and feel of England. Roads cut across green fields. Canals crisscrossed them. Railways swept through them. And buildings of all kinds packed on to land which once was countryside. Aggressive, coarse, brash and bold, the burgeoning towns swallowed up land and suffocated the old society. It seemed that deference was overcome by antagonism, that respect for order was defeated by rebelliousness, that hierarchical attitudes were overwhelmed by class loyalties.

The great towns and cities were frightening. In particular, upper- and middle-class people shrank from the gathering of working-class people in populous districts. These were heavy with unhealthy smells. They were dark from the smoke which billowed from factory chimneys, from the crowding of houses which seemed to push out fresh air and light, and from too few street lamps. In the frantic imagination of many upper- and middle-class- people, they appeared to be foreign places full of danger, disease and debauchery.

This gloomy and depressing picture was reinforced by novels like George Gissing's *The Nether World*. Published in 1889, it was infused with pessimism and loathing of the urban poor. These features were made plain in Gissing's account of 'a disagreeable quarter, a street of squalid houses, swarming with yet more squalid children'. On all the doorsteps sat little girls, 'themselves only just out of infancy, nursing or neglecting bald, red-eyed, doughy-limbed abortions in every stage of babyhood, hapless spawn of diseased humanity, born to embitter and brutalize yet further the lot of those who unwillingly gave them life'. Even sympathetic observers viewed the slum as an abyss in which physical and moral degradation was rife. This term was used by General William Booth of the Salvation Army, by the novelist Jack London, and by the future Liberal minister C. F. G. Masterman.

But to insiders, urban working-class districts were not hells: they were villages and they were neighbourhoods. In 1856 a journalist called Hugh Shimmin entered an insanitary and tumbledown court in Oriel Street, Liverpool. He asked some of the inhabitants 'why they remained in such wretched places, as, for a few pence more each week, which might be saved from the grog-shop, they could get much better residences, and in a more healthy situation'. One old woman 'stepped forward to reply'. She had lived in the court for a long time and she had found friends and neighbours there. As she put it 'a neighbour was not easy to be met with in any place or every day, and it was not easy to leave a spot which she had known so long, and where, in sorrow or in joy, she had met with sympathetic hearts'.

Close-knit communities such as this arose because migrants to a particular town or city had much in common. Most of them came from the surrounding rural villages. An investigation of Blackburn showed that between 1850 and 1870, families moving into the town travelled an average distance of five miles per generation. An equivalent situation was obvious in the poor district of Summer Lane, Birmingham. In 1881 in the back-to-back courtyards which lay off the road, 75% of the population was born in the city. The great majority of the rest came from the encircling counties of Warwickshire, Worcestershire and Staffordshire. As a result of local migration, many newcomers had similar backgrounds and they spoke the same accent and dialect. Towns and cities were entrenched in their wider hinterland; they were not separated from them.

The movement of people from certain areas to one place in particular was as noticeable amongst ethnic minorities. Jenifer Davis[1] has showed that in the 1860s in Jennings' Buildings, Kensington, many of the Irish inhabitants were linked 'by ties of kinship and other connections which had their roots in Cork'. In the same manner, most of the Italians in Birmingham's Digbeth district came from villages by the town of Sora, lying between Rome and Naples. Through intermarriage, many of them were related. These ties became more pronounced after their emigration, and they led to the formation of large kinship networks like that of the Tavoliers, Boves, Gregos and Sartoris.

Comparable patterns of immigration are as evident in the late twentieth century. Birmingham has a large number of South Asian Moslems. Many of them are born and bred in the city, but their parents are mostly from Punjab and Kashmir. The majority of the Punjabis are from Rawalpindi or Gujar Khan, whilst the greater part of the Kashmiris come from Mirpur. And most of the Mirpuris are from the two tehsirs of Dhadyal and Khadanvad. Similarly, the majority of the city's Irish are from Roscommon, Sligo, Mayo and Dublin; most of the Bangla Deshis are from Syllhet; and most of the Afro-Caribbeans are from Barbados and Jamaica.

Many of these immigrants have settled in distinct areas, seeking the support of kin and neighbours; they have created stable yet lively communities. So did the English, Italian, Jewish and Irish people who moved into the towns and cities of nineteenth-century Britain. Robert Roberts grew up in the Hope Street district of Salford, where the population was generally immobile by the early 1900s. He observed that 'fifty years before, our area had horrified even Friedrich Engels, and Engels knew a slum when he saw one'. Since then 'many of the vilest hovels had been swept away', but 'here, if anywhere on earth, when darkness fell, lay the "city of the dreadful night" '.

But Hope Street was not the city of the dreadful night. Nor was it an abyss. It was a thriving locality with its own facilities. Roberts underlined these features in *The Classic Slum,* probably the most perceptive working-class autobiography which has been written. He discerned that his own district was not unusual, arguing that every industrial city 'folds within itself a clutter of loosely-defined overlapping "villages" '. His own had about three thousand inhabitants living in 'some thirty streets and alleys'. It was marked off to the north and south by railway lines; to the west, beyond the tram lines, 'lay the middle classes, bay-windowed and begardened', and to the east was 'another slum'.

The Nichol in London was another clearly defined urban village. Its boundaries were High Street Shoreditch and Hackney Road on the north, and Spitalfields to the south. Unlike Hope Street, the Nichol had its own major shopping thoroughfare. Arthur Harding proclaimed that Church Street was 'the high heaven' of everything in the district. It had pubs like the 'Crown' where the bird fanciers met, 'a big men's and boy's tailor's shop called Lynn's', a fish and chip shop, a timber yard, a coffee house, a wet-fish shop, a Salvation Army Chapel, several wardrobe dealers', a chemist 'who sold every kind of medicines and cures for every kind of illness', a pork butcher which was 'the best in the locality', a doctor's shop, a barber, a baker, a corner shop which was 'a God-send to the hungry children of the district' because it sold large bags of broken biscuits for a halfpenny or a penny, an undertaker, numerous food shops, a soup kitchen, a rag-and-bone shop, a grocer's 'selling very cheap tea, sugar, etc.', and a pudding shop which charged a penny for hot pies and a portion of jam roly-poly.

It is significant that Church Street ran into Shoreditch High Street. In this way the Nichol was connected to a wider area. It was not shut off and isolated: it was embedded within Bethnal Green and Shoreditch. Both these places were the size of towns. So were Portsea in Portsmouth, Ancoats in Manchester, and Duddeston and Nechells in Birmingham. By 1871 this latter place had a population of about 46,000. It was separated from adjoining townships in the city by clear boundaries: from Aston Cross by the Birmingham to Fazeley Canal; from Saltley and Bordesley by railway lines; and from Digbeth by two main roads, Dartmouth and Lawley Streets. Duddeston occupied the southern part of the town. Within this area, two villages stood out. Vauxhall was cut off by railway lines and was home to many regularly employed railwaymen and their families. To its west, Ashted was characterized by back-to-back housing and a mainly poorer population. But both villages were brought together by the major shopping centre of Great Lister Street. This was also 'the monkey run', the road along which boys and girls walked with their 'pals' on a Saturday or Sunday night. Their hope was 'to click' with someone of the opposite sex.

Shoreditch High Street had the same functions. Harding called it the local 'Champs Elyseé'. It was 'a prosperous market place with stalls and shops on both sides of the street', and it boasted the 'London' music hall as well as many pubs. Elsewhere in the East End, 'The Lane' in Whitechapel was another focal point. For Elizabeth Flint[2] a trip there was 'one of the peaks of our existence'. Along Whitechapel Road there were hawkers selling oranges, 'Fatty White' calling out 'whelks and cockles and winkles', and a 'hot chestnut barrow on the roadway that led into the Lane' itself. This was full of stalls 'side by side, and noise and light were tossed together, a noise that had a quality of heaviness all made up of talking and screaming and laughing, yet with no part of it separate and on its own'. In the winter the Lane was lit by naphtha flares which were 'forever leaping and hissing like chained dogs that cannot escape the kennel to which they are tied'. Nothing was still: people were moving all the time, and it seemed there was such a friendliness and 'such a happiness that no one could ever find today'.

Many urban villages were not as distinct as the Nichol or Hope Street. Lying off the main shopping thoroughfares, they faded imperceptibly into one another. Still, working-class people knew their own patch, their own end. The size of this space was flexible, and it was affected by a number of factors such as age, gender, work and leisure interests. But it was clear that the lives of poorer people revolved round a smaller area than did those of the better off. This interpretation is indicated by the research of Hugh McLeod.[3] Concentrating on the later 1800s he examined the marriage patterns in four London parishes: St John's, Paddington was a wealthy locality; St Mary's, Lewisham was a middle-class district; St Andrew's, Bethnal Green was made up mostly of skilled workers and their families; and in St Clement's, Notting Hill the unskilled were in the majority. Within these parishes McLeod identified neighbourhoods. These were less than half a mile square, they were not crossed by railways, waterways or main roads, and they were not broken up by parks or a belt of factories. In the poorest parish, 82% of men married someone from their own neighbourhood. This compared to 65% in the upper-working-class district, 25% in the middle-class locality and just 20% in the rich area.

McLeod's work is important because it gives a shape to the space which was below the urban village. A similar impression can be gained by an examination of the moves of poorer families. David R. Green and Alan G. Parton[4] studied slum areas in London and Birmingham during the mid-1800s. In all of them 'there existed a shiftless sub-strata of tramps and vagrants who moved from place to place and lodging-house to lodging-house', people who passed through the community but were not part of it. But for the rest of the inhabitants 'residential mobility took place often within tightly circumscribed spatial limits'. This contention is supported by other research. Michael Anderson[5] noticed that in one area of Preston in 1861 almost 40% of men 'were found in the same house or within 200 yards of the house that they had occupied ten years earlier'. It was probable that 'another 10–20% were living within less than half a mile'. Lynn Lees[6] discovered similar instances amongst Irish families in London in the 1850s. Some of these moved several times between Bermondsey and Southwark. On all occasions, however, their residences were within 'one half-mile at most' of their previous home.

The movements of most poor people were circular. My great-uncle Bill recalled that in the 1890s and early 1900s his family rented various houses in Sparkbrook, Birmingham:

We left out of White Street to go to Studley Street. We knocked on the landlord there. Studley Street we went to Moseley Road. When we got to Moseley Road Mom had bought me a long pair of trousers. I was only twelve and her said, 'Goo and gerra job. Tell 'em y're fourteen'. I went out and got a job in no time. Got a job in Conybere Street. Eight bob a week. Then we come from Moseley Road back into Brunswick Road, worn it? Then Stoney Lane where you get on the bus and then into Queen Street . . . Alfred Street. Back to Studley Street back of Duggin's, Greenway's. Then from Greenway's we went back into Alfred Street.

Over about a fifteen-year period, my great-uncle lived in nine houses. Seven of them were within 100 yards of his first home in White Street. A. S. Jasper had a comparable experience in London. He thought that he had never heard of a family who 'moved more than we did'. Like the Chinns, they 'flitted' regularly when they fell into arrears with their rent. But until 1919 their changes of address were within a small area between Essex Road and Hackney Road. Significantly, all were within half a mile of Hoxton Street, where the Jaspers sometimes had a market stall.

Outsiders found it difficult to recognize these amorphous neighbourhoods, but insiders were acutely aware of them, and there were facilities which acted as linchpins. Chief of these were small corner shops. These were more than an essential economic facility: they played a vital role as a meeting-place, and they connected one street to another. In this way, individual streets coalesced to become part of a neighbourhood. Corner and back street pubs performed the same function. My great-uncle Wal Chinn emphasized that it was unusual to find strangers in 'the local'. They were used by regulars 'who remained loyal to their chosen meeting-place'. His dad's pub was in Studley Street, yet it was more than a drinking establishment. 'The Gate' had a football team in the local league and it was the focus for the celebration of major events in the life of the street and the nation.

Standish Meacham[7] proposed that neighbourhood meant more than houses and streets. It meant 'the mutually beneficial relationship one formed with others; a sort of social symbiosis'. Elizabeth Roberts[8] agreed with this general statement, but she qualified her support. She argued that urban villages lacked 'a structure through which communal action could be channelled', and that they were too large for people to feel they knew everyone. Her research focused on Barrow, Lancaster and Preston. In these places 'what seems to have been of considerably greater importance to working-class people was the street, or possibly the small group of streets, in which they lived'.

There is not any tension between this assertion and my argument that the lives of working-class people overlapped into spatial communities of different sizes. This contention is supported by the example of 'The Lane' area of Sparkbrook, a generally upper-working-class town in Birmingham. It was marked out by a railway line to the west, by main roads to the north and east, and by two smaller roads to the south. Internally, it was united by the Ladypool Road, described by Leslie Mayell[9] as a 'vital and pulsating' artery. It had 'everything' – 'a rich variety of shops', pubs, a picture house, a chapel, a church, a park, a school and 'probably other things that do not immediately come to my mind'.

The township of 'The Lane' was split into two villages by Highgate Road. In turn these manifested a number of neighbourhoods. One of them was made up of Alfred, Queen and Studley Streets. This was seen as a poor quarter, and it had a population of about a thousand. Within it, Studley Street was regarded as the poorest part. This was just 200 yards in length and in 1891 it had a population of 408 living in 81 houses. The street was infamous as 'the worst' in the area, and it was feared as a place where 'no copper would go down on his own'. But Studley Street was not a ghetto. One end ran on to the Ladypool Road, and the other was connected to Queen Street by a 'huckster's shop' – a corner shop which was open all hours and sold everything. Nor were its people an undifferentiated mass of the poor: they formed a heterogeneous community. Most of the men 'were ordinary factory chaps, builders, labourers and anybody 'as had rough and ready jobs', but they lived alongside a publican, a coalyard owner, a baker, and two small shopkeepers.

Many of the street's people were related to each other. Between 1908 and 1910 it had five families called Warwick, three each named Jones and Stokes, and two each with the surnames of Moore, Reeves, Chambers, Harris, Hyde, Beedon, Bashford, Parton and Fawkes. The connections between the local families were enhanced by intermarriage. In the eight years from 1906, fourteen people from the street were married at the local Church of England. In ten cases their partners were also from Studley Street; in three others, the partner was from an adjoining street; and in the last instance, the partner was from the next district. The ties of blood meant that Studley Street and its people became one and the same thing. This led to a staunch loyalty which was evident in many poor streets throughout urban England. Such an attachment was strengthened because the street was 'the great recreation room' of the slums. Children played on it, mothers met there as they went to shop, young men gathered on its corners, bookies stood on it taking bets, and women sat on their steps watching the comings and goings. The activities of the street were crucial for socializing. Significantly, they were free.

To some outsiders the gathering of the poor on the street was intimidating; to others it symbolized the new race of 'pavement folk'. But for the poor the street was a vital place. Compared to their decayed and overcrowded homes it was spacious, lively and exhilarating. More than this, in a country which denied them so much, it belonged to them. But the street was not the smallest spatial community amongst the poor. Over one hundred people could live in a terrace of back-to-backs. Their immediate world was that of the yard and its facilities, which they all shared. In particular, this space was important for young children, the old, and women who worked at home.

This is shown clearly by numerous photographs in Birmingham Library Services 'Slum Collection'. In Studley Street one yard was known as 'Carey's', because so many members of that family lived in the same terrace. Elsewhere, there were similar instances of relatives gathering especially close to each other. Basil and Ellen Sanders lived in 'the badly overcrowded' Princes Court, Bethnal Green. Ellen's mother lived next door and probably she 'had recommended or "spoken for them" to the rent collector'. The other families in the court did the same. This meant that Mrs Field and Mrs Ricketts were sisters. So too were Mrs Sullivan and Mrs Barney, Mrs Mabley and Mrs Collins, Mrs Gray and Mrs Shepherd, and Mrs Cook, Mrs Main and Mrs Newman. As this example highlighted, the English poor were distinguished not only by their endogamy but also by their matrilocality. This meant that a married couple was more likely to live near the family of the wife. There was a good reason for this. Wives and mothers were in the forefront of the daily battle against poverty. They needed each other's help – and family and kin were more likely to give assistance than were strangers.

Working-class neighbourhoods and villages were not nether worlds; they were organic communities. But most planners, councillors, officials and commentators were oblivious to their existence. This meant that solutions to the problems of bad housing and an unhealthy environment were imposed from above. The views and experiences of working-class people were not sought by the authorities. Redevelopment stormed through their areas: it destroyed their shopping thoroughfares; it obliterated their corner shops and pubs; it shattered their overlapping communities; it disenfranchised them because it took away their independence and their self-help. But people are resilient. They have continued to bond together in neighbourhoods, villages and towns. They continue to know their ends and to help each other within them. Now local and central governments have an opportunity to notice these communities and to give them power. They must listen to the voices from below. They have to be alert to the boundaries within each city – boundaries which are not reflected by municipal wards or parliamentary constituencies. They need to realize that people live within overlapping spaces. They must be aware of the importance of shopping facilities. They ought to realize that power and authority have to be given to smaller units of government. And they must acknowledge that these units must be determined from below.

National government ought to devolve more power and authority to the elected authorities of great towns and cities. These bodies should be responsible for global matters. In turn, these larger units should recognize their constituent townships and allow them to have their own councils, made up of representatives from the urban villages of each town. These councils should have the power and money to do what local people want. They should be able to pay for local police stations and local police officers; for park keepers; for skips and for cleansing; for pavement repairs; for neighbourhood caretakers; for crèche and play-scheme workers; for the establishment and upkeep of neighbourhood offices and urban village community centres; for the Development Trusts which Anita Halliday described and for whatever is important to local residents.

Notes and references

1. Davis, J., in D. Feldman and G.S. Johns (1989) *Metropolis London: Histories and Representation Since 1800*. London: Routledge.
2. Flint, E. (1963) *Hot Bread and Chips*. London: Museum Press.
3. McLeod, H. (1974) *Class and Religion in the late Victorian City*. Longman.
4. Green, D.R. and Parton, G. 'Slums and Slum Life in Victorian England', in M. Gastrell, (ed.) (1990) *Slums*. Leicester: Leicester University Press.
5. Anderson, M. (1971) *Family Structure in Nineteenth Century Lancashire*. London: Longman.
6. Lees, L. (1969) *Social Change and Stability among the London Irish*. Harvard University: PhD Thesis.
7. Meacham, S. (1977) *A Life Apart: The English Working Class, 1890–1914*. London.
8. Roberts, E. (1985) *A Woman's Place: An Oral History of Working Class Women, 1840–1940*. Oxford: Blackwell.
9. Mayell, L. (1980) *The Birmingham I Remember*. Padistow: Lodenak Press.

10

PLANNING FOR REAL LIFE

Joe Holyoak

For two decades, from about 1955 to 1975, the inner areas of Britain's cities were subjected to a programme of doctrinaire replanning and redevelopment. Before redevelopment, as Carl Chinn describes, these areas were typically composed of a network of streets, filled with densely packed terraces of small houses, mixed together with industry, rows of shops, corner pubs, schools and churches. This fabric was essentially the product of the boom years of the late nineteenth century, when industrial cities had grown enormously. These areas were unplanned, lacking in green open spaces, and much of the housing was unsanitary and deficient in construction. Huge numbers of working-class families lived in these poor conditions. But the environment had some compensating virtues: it was cheap, it was neighbourly and it was convenient for the city centre and other facilities. It was a hard environment and perhaps we should not regret its passing too much. But today it seems like a totally departed world.

The doctrine behind the redevelopment was heavily influenced by the ideas of Le Corbusier and his contemporaries but usually flavoured by an English picturesqueness. It resulted typically in a drastic reduction in residential density (often from about four hundred people per hectare to about two hundred and fifty) and in an environment in which the familiar streets had disappeared and been replaced by a mixture of high-, medium- and low-rise housing placed among green public spaces. Through the method of compulsory purchase, the industry had mainly been moved out and the variety of privately-owned shops and other facilities replaced by council-owned facilities grouped in local centres. Middle-class residents such as teachers and doctors, who may have owned their own houses, were often moved out too, as the compulsory purchase process was not discriminating, resulting in a uniform, single class, single use, urban environment.

In few historical times or places has development or redevelopment been so sudden and cataclysmic. It was done with the best of intentions on the part of government ministers, local authority councillors, town planners and architects, who believed they were building a new, better post-war society. It was also done with at least the passive support of many of the residents, who, seeped in the culture of dependence, believed the propaganda and trusted that the experts knew what they were doing.

However, from the advantage of the perspective of the present day, we can see that there were two main deficiencies in this process.

First, the new principles of urban design on which the redevelopment was based were untested and mistaken.

Second, the residents of the redevelopment areas were treated simply as consumers who had no choice; the experts knew what was good for them and the residents had no say in the way in which their familiar environments were destroyed and replaced.

A feature of the 1980s and 1990s in British cities is the way in which these redevelopment areas built in the 1960s and 1970s are being redesigned in an attempt to correct both these major historical mistakes.

At the same time that the redesign of the estates built in the 1960s and 1970s has become an accepted and conventional process, similar processes of improvement have been applied to the pre-1914 housing areas of the inner city which escaped comprehensive redevelopment. These areas are composed of streets of terraced houses which were not categorized as slums but which are now often in need of environmental upgrading. Although built at a fairly high density, they have an advantage over the redeveloped estates of the 1960s and 1970s because all the dwellings have a front door at ground level, possess a garden and the layout of the streets is comprehensible and legible.

This is in contrast to the patterns of layout that we typically find in a redeveloped area. The street network that connected the whole area was replaced by disconnected super blocks, fragmenting the area into separate estates. Plenty of open green space was provided but mostly of a featureless, unfriendly, kind that is pleasant to look at from the tower blocks but is not very usable and is often positively unsafe. The legible, secure and neighbourly space of the street was replaced by a confusing and unsafe tangle of courtyards and cul-de-sacs. At least half the dwellings are likely to be above ground level, with no private outdoor space. The convenient landmarks of corner shops and pubs disappeared altogether, creating a monotonous and uniform landscape.

As an architect and urban designer, I have worked with residents on area regeneration projects both in redeveloped estates and in older housing areas. Common to all of them has been the active participation of residents in the planning and decision-taking process. We believe that part of the reason why so many important mistakes were made in the design of new estates in the 1960s and 1970s was that residents had no involvement in the process – they were treated as passive recipients, mere consumers of the products of the professionals, who themselves were often detached from and ignorant about the lives of the people whose environment they were radically rebuilding.

We have learnt that if ordinary 'inexpert' people are given the confidence that improvement really will happen, provided with the resources with which to plan, and offered accessible expert advice to help them make decisions, then they are eager and capable of deciding what needs to happen to improve their environment and how it could be done. There has been considerable agreement between residents about the content of the improvement schemes. People who live in a particular place have a shared experience of what it is like to live there and of what needs doing to make it better; it is they who are the experts. So it is the job of the professionals to listen to what they say and to translate it into a process by which the improvements can be realized.

A recognized vocabulary of participation techniques has developed which are in regular use by community architects and which can help to enable a community to take decisions about the improvement or redesign of its own area. 'Planning for Real' is a well-known technique, invented by Tony Gibson of the Neighbourhood Initiatives Foundation. The name is frequently misused to become almost a synonym for community participation. It is in fact a very flexible device which entails building a large scale model of the area to enable large numbers of people in a meeting or series of meetings to contribute their different ideas about improvement in a highly efficient and synthesized way. There are design workshops – concentrated sessions with a group of residents making decisions about layout and improvement, again making use of simple, moveable models. On a larger scale, there is the planning weekend, a highly structured and intensive event in which the energies and abilities of a large number of residents can be marshalled to produce proposals on which there can be a consensus of agreement.

These techniques have become part of a new orthodoxy of community-based design. Yet, though experience in using them is necessary if they are to be successful, they are all characterized by being essentially simple and accessible ways of allowing people to become aware of what the problems are, knowing what can be done about them and agreeing on how to do it as harmoniously as possible. Techniques can become more complex if it is necessary. For example, in the replanning of the Pype Hayes Estate in Birmingham, which involves rebuilding 1500 houses and rehousing most of the residents, we invented a model-based technique called PHASE (Pype Hayes Allocation Simulation Exercise) which residents used to decide where they were moving to and to work out how the large number of moves could be co-ordinated.

We have learnt not to place too much importance on architectural style, that area where architects normally believe they have the right to impose their own strange ideas. Our clients are usually conservative when it comes to the appearance of their dwellings – they just want them to look like everyone else's dwellings and they certainly do not want to be patronized. There was an unpleasant incident in the inner city area of Ladywood in Birmingham when an executive architect, directing a contract based upon the residents' brief which we had co-ordinated, had balconies on a block of maisonettes painted in loud and varied colours. The residents felt that the architect was amusing himself at their expense, and at considerable cost the balconies were repainted in more sober colours.

In these area improvement schemes, we usually find ourselves working in collaboration with a number of local authority departments. We have learnt that, though they can be effective at tackling their own individual and specialist agenda of housing, roads, leisure, education and so on, council departments are not very good at working together to produce a co-ordinated plan for a neighbourhood as a whole. They suffer from over-specialization and failure to see how the overall community functions. Despite the considerable resources of staff and finance that the local authority possesses we, as employees of the residents, have often found that we can move much more quickly and think more holistically. We are unrestricted by departmental boundaries and therefore maintain the initiative in moving the project along in a consolidated way. Moreover, because the council's departments are each responsible for only one subject and the responsibility for co-ordinating them often appears to be uncertainly located, we have often found ourselves adopting the co-ordination role ourselves, although this was not a role we are usually paid to do.

This co-ordinating role is of course one of the definitions of what an urban designer does and we always act using an urban design perspective. In area regeneration projects, this involves two related objectives

The first is to co-ordinate all the various initiatives – housing improvement, new housing, traffic management, open space improvement, commercial development, etc. – so that they do not remain separate items but work together to result in a harmonized environment. Without an urban design perspective this harmony rarely results. Yet, reasonably enough, residents expect the local authority to act in a corporate manner and find it difficult to understand that fragmented, departmental specialism results in disharmony and lack of interpretation. The residents' expectations are quite legitimate. It suggests that the consolidating role should normally be played by urban designers employed by residents, not councils.

The second objective is perhaps the more important one, but it is correspondingly more difficult to achieve. When working in a comprehensively redeveloped area such as Ladywood, one of the starting points for the urban design analysis is to look back to the pre-redevelopment fabric and identify the positive qualities it possessed which have been lost. These usually include such qualities as connectivity, legibility, conveniently mixed land uses and the variety of commercial and social facilities that a high residential density can support. Top-down planning had displaced these initial, integrated qualities with disconnection and severance, disaggregation, land use zoning, a thinly spread residential density and a shortage of all kinds of facilities, thus reducing the quality of life in the neighbourhood.

In an inner-city area which has not been comprehensively redeveloped on modernist lines, these alien qualities do not dominate, but neither are they entirely absent. In an area like Balsall Heath in Birmingham, which consists mainly of the original byelaw street development, planning changes have been made which have eroded the area's integrity. Sections of new housing development replacing the old have been built which use suburban patterns, weakening street enclosure, facing away from streets. The connectivity of the street layout has been damaged, with streets made into cul-de-sacs. A bypass has taken through traffic off the main road. This has resulted in a once thriving section of a local shopping centre becoming isolated and blighted. Residents warned that this would happen but nobody in 'authority' listened to this 'inexpert' voice.

Both new and old areas require urban design codes to be drawn up which can guide future change and development along lines which encourage an environment which is lively, safe, stimulating and legible, which feels like the home it really is to so many people. For Ladywood we drew up a set of 12 rules for our urban design study. Many of these summarize a reversal of the principles which were dominant in the 1960s. They concern such matters as the placing of buildings in relationship to each other, the overcoming of severance caused by wide dual carriageway roads, the relationship of buildings to public open space and the permeability and legibility of the routes network. They may not all fit the needs of other areas but nevertheless we believe they do possess a degree of common currency. The twelve rules are:

• Traffic calming is to be introduced where necessary.
• Buildings should as far as possible form streets.
• Old buildings are to be integrated with the new development.
• Opportunities are to be taken to create more defensible local spaces.
• Unpopular pedestrian subways which 'belong' to no one are to be removed.
• Local places are to be enhanced by environmental improvements.
• Buildings should have mixed uses where appropriate.
• Premises should possess comprehensible addresses.
• New buildings are to be figurative in composition.
• Ground floors of buildings should generate activity and ownership.
• Public open spaces are to have enclosing edges, clear boundaries.
• The network of routes is to have continuity and conform to existing, commonsense usage.

We were encouraged that the general policy contained in these rules – which can be summarized as 'reurbanization' – is echoed in the European Union's 1990 Green Paper on the Urban Environment. This too condemns the fragmented, zoned and dispersed localities that were built in the 1960s and encourages the re-establishment of many older, more traditional principles of urban design – principles that have been tested over hundreds of years and whose robustness has been proved.

We are encouraged also by the fact that in general our new (or is it old?) principles of urban design coincide with residents' descriptions of the kind of environment in which they want to live. However, tensions and contradictions between our views and those of the residents for whom we work do occur and need to be seen as a constructive debate between partners, even between employers and skilled employees. An example is residents' resistance to proposals to build new houses on underused pieces of green space. Although the benefits of a higher residential density – a livelier, safer public realm; more shops and facilities which can be supported; local schools made more viable – are agreed in principle, there is great attachment to grass and trees and a reluctance to see them disappear. The debate about issues such as these is a valuable and ongoing part of a community-based regeneration process, provided we remember who is the employer and who is the employee. We are free to offer our view and give reasons, but ultimately it is the people who have to live with and maintain the design who must decide.

Community architecture, advocacy planning, or whatever one calls it, is often characterized by those ignorant of it or opposed to it as simply a facile process of 'giving people what they want'. It is not that simple. Even if the members of a community are mostly in agreement about the sort of environment in which they want to live, there will still be plenty of contradictions between the needs of that community and the interests and activities of the wider community in which it sits. These will be expressed in arguments over such diverse things as pressures for commercial development, issues of crime, through traffic, housing allocations policy and out-of-town shopping. A community-based regeneration programme has to combine the participatory process of discussion and decision-taking with a debate about the complex urban design issues which shape the character of the place and which can resolve the differences between local and regional needs.

It is becoming increasingly accepted as conventional wisdom that a dialogue between professionals and local people, with the community possessing the power to write its own agenda, is the only satisfactory way to plan and regenerate local urban areas – that the elitist way in which such processes were done in the past was misguided then and is obsolete now. But the benefits of this are not only in physical environments which are made to fit their occupants. Through the experience of a regeneration process, a large number of residents who were once passive recipients, have become active citizens who think and take decisions about the form and nature of the place where they live. The collective effect of that social change is incalculable but it must be considerable. Certainly, it makes for a robust community which has been shaped by the people who live in it.

11

THE SOCIAL ENTREPRENEUR

Inger Boyett and Don Finlay

In Victorian Britain the school head teacher along with other local officials was seen as a pivotal force in the economic development of an area. This recognition has declined over time and increasingly in the last decade when the policy-makers have been denigrating the outcomes of the state school sector to facilitate policy changes. A number of academics have identified the role of the 'community entrepreneur' in local economic development. This chapter, using the case of a school situated in a depressed area of Nottinghamshire and its head teacher, attempts to examine the role of the head teacher as a 'community entrepreneur'. The study would seem to suggest that entrepreneurial head teachers may provide a more cost-effective input in the long-term generation of depressed areas, than high levels of finance or artificially created community entrepreneurs in the form of civil servant consultants.

A definition for the community entrepreneur might be developed as:

- a leader who displays entrepreneurial characteristics within any organization and who encourages the development of these characteristics in others;
- an individual who helps new entrepreneurs acquire an enhanced level of self-confidence and develop enterprising skills, such as alertness, awareness and recognition of the benefits of profit gain;
- a manager in a successful entrepreneurial organization who provides a role model for new entrepreneurs to emulate; and
- an entrepreneur who has not only developed large direct and indirect networks but is also generous in sharing these networks with new entrepreneurs.

Nottinghamshire is a county in the East Midlands of England made up of three distinct types of area: the urbanized, relatively affluent south around the county town of Nottingham; the agricultural east; and the northern end of the county, home of the Nottinghamshire coalfields. Mansfield, only some twelve miles from Nottingham, is the gateway town to the numerous colliery villages, including Clipstone, scattered across northern Nottinghamshire and South Yorkshire, which like the rest of the UK coal industry, has been contracting over the last twenty years and is nearing extinction. Very little replacement industry has been attracted to the area, and unemployment in 1993 was running at 14.8% against the national average of 12.2%.

The Garibaldi School, built in Clipstone in the late 1960s to accommodate 1100 pupils aged between 11 and 18, is sited next to a large council estate close to a number of coal pits, all of which have since closed. Over 90% of the children within its catchment area come from working-class homes. Like all state secondary schools in the UK, Garibaldi had been subjected to changes introduced by the 1988 Education Act. The Local Management of Schools (LMS) resulted in a reduction in the influence of local education authorities (LEA); budgets and management were devolved to the control of schools themselves; competition was developed between local schools through parental choices and examination league tables; and the emphasis was placed on 'quality' education. In 1993 there were 800 pupils attending Garibaldi School, with a rise to 1000 predicted in the next two years and a current teaching staff of 45.

The school was managed until his retirement in 1989 by a head teacher, who had held his post for nearly twenty years. He had developed a hierarchical structure within the organization, with the head teacher at the pinnacle, three deputy heads, heads and deputy heads of faculty, heads of department and, in some cases, deputy heads of department, and finally the other teaching staff. The pastoral care side of the organization was managed again through a hierarchical structure of year heads, deputy year heads and class tutors.

In 1989 a new head teacher was appointed, Bob Salisbury, who moved from a school in an affluent suburb on the outskirts of Nottingham city. Despite having other available headships which he could have pursued, his first interview was at Garibaldi School where he was stimulated by '. . . the chance to take a school that was down at heel and see if you can bring it up quite quickly'. He also had the feeling that it would be more challenging to start from such a low point and that it would possibly prove an 'easier' management task than moving a school up from a middle ranking position.

On arrival at the school, Bob talked to parents, staff and children with the objective of finding out about his new school; very quickly he discovered just how low the school's perceived image was. The consensus seemed that it was an 'ugly' kind of school, it was rough and not one to which parents would voluntarily send their children. Within the local community the school was seen as impoverished as the surrounding area itself. There was little expectation that it would either provide the local children with a route to an economically enhanced adulthood, or encourage any economic regeneration of the local area.

Bob himself was well aware of the link between the school and the problems in the economic community surrounding it. Very early in his leadership at Garibaldi's, Bob was also made acutely aware of the need for the school to generate resources above and beyond what it received from the local education authority. 'Somebody came to me one day and asked for £200 for technical equipment and we didn't have it. Suddenly this vision came of it being the same in ten years' time unless I did something about it. You were never going to get a budget to enable you to do all the things you wanted to do. You were never going to get a budget to recruit the best staff. That was the impetus.'

Discussions with staff had firmed up Bob's initial feelings of staff demoralization. 'The public image and the reputation were demoralizing in themselves, but much more important than that, the lid had never been lifted from these people. There was a culture that meant that people would not have a cup of tea without asking for permission.' An organizational culture change was obviously needed as badly as a marketing initiative.

Cultural change at Garibaldi School

Bob's first move was to initiate an open-door policy: '. . . his door is always open and not just for us; the kids as well can go in and talk to him quite freely'.

When Bob took over the management of Garibaldi there were already in place 'rules' relating to the culture of the establishment, for example that everyone should be treated with dignity and respect. One of his first changes was to put into practice what had previously only been written statements: 'If you are treating the pupils with dignity and respect, why are they banned from being in the school buildings at break and lunchtimes? If you are trying to get them to grow into responsible adults, how can you equate that with saying to them as soon as the bell goes, "Everyone out"?' Despite doubts by some members of the staff about the safety of the premises with unsupervised children wandering around, in fact Bob's initiative was rewarded with the removal of a level of tension. The pupils, now feeling trusted, responded with responsible behaviour, whilst the staff were no longer conscious of the stresses caused by maintaining a 'siege' within the buildings at break times. Additionally, rather than damage to the premises increasing, it was reduced dramatically to become almost non-existent.

With one area of the pupil/staff relationship improved, Bob turned his attention to the demoralization from which the staff team appeared to be suffering. They seemed not only reticent in making moves without explicit instructions from Bob, but the culture which seemed to have developed under the previous head teacher was, as Bob describes it, a 'punishment culture'. The staff were demotivated from initiating any innovative projects because of what might happen if their projections or assumptions were wrong. Through staff discussion, Bob attempted to introduce the feeling that '. . . mistakes are good; if you try something and it doesn't quite work, you are not hauled on the mat any more. Instead you get a pat on the back for having a bash; inertia is the greatest sin.'

Using a bobbing cork analogy, Bob persuaded the staff, through the development of the three- and five-year plans, that the whole team was actively trying to flow in the same direction towards the same shared outcomes and that at any one time, because of special initiatives or need, one or other of the corks might be popping up to float higher in the water, only to sink down to the same level as all the others later on. Using his increased control of salary payments, Bob used the monies available to reward his staff to match the system of short-term high profile activity in particular areas. Rather than promotions or permanent increases in salary, he initiated a system of floating payments and responsibility allowances restricted to time periods, such as a school term. By tying down targets for the individuals receiving the extra payments he also developed a system of reward which could be linked to the annual appraisal system. '. . . The money is nice, but it isn't that which gets people going, it is the trust that you are offering to them, the reward for the initiative and the fact that if it doesn't work you won't be castigated. If it does, that's a bonus for all of us.'

The marketing of Garibaldi School

Following a discussion meeting with staff it was decided that Bob would approach a local industrialist to attempt to gain assistance in their task. The managing director of the local Mansfield Breweries, Ron Kirk, was a member of the school's governing board and the majority decision was to approach him first. 'We were lucky in that the first person I approached was a very enlightened industrialist. The minute I started talking to him he said they would do everything they could to support us. He understood the need for youngsters in a fairly impoverished area – this is not Latin-primer country here – and we were lucky that he picked up on our needs quickly.' Ron Kirk suggested that Bob should arrange to see Mansfield Breweries' marketing consultants, Miles Communication in Nottingham, to talk through with them possible marketing strategies. Using his business contacts and calling in 'favours', Ron Kirk arranged a 'free' day, where the directors at Miles Communication talked Bob through the basic rules and strategies for marketing. 'It was quite honestly fascinating. A lot of the things we now churn out are directly attributable to that first talk with the marketing company.'

The need, emphasized by the marketing company, to provide good communication links with the parents was particularly difficult in the early days, when parents' evenings would be lucky to draw an audience of thirty people. The newsletters and feature articles negotiated in the local newspaper were the initial tools used to generate interest in the school amongst the more apathetic parents. In an attempt to gain quickly a greater understanding of the perceptions and needs of these and every other stakeholder in Garibaldi that could be identified, Bob sent out a questionnaire with just two questions:

1. What do you think of Garibaldi School?
2. When you choose a school, what do you look for?

'We sent them to every parent, local politicians and MPs. We took them down to the Miners' Welfare and I talked to anybody who would listen. We took them to the local education officers, to the Chamber of Commerce and to as many companies as we could think of.' This was probably the point at which Bob Salisbury started to widen his organizational structure, enlarging the web to encompass the community at large. A network was in the first stages of formation.

The results were depressing in relation to Question 1: Garibaldi did not feature highly in most people's perceptions. The responses to Question 2 proved more productive, allowing the school to identify about twenty common characteristics of choice. Bob and his team were able to identify 18 on which they felt they could have some influence, and using these points as guides, the school management team developed a mission statement linked to timescales, a three- and a five-year school plan and strategies for implementation.

We wrote a marketing plan and we linked that to the school plan for the next three years. The marketing plan was really an extraction from the school development plan. In it we put things like: we need to have roadshows in the primary schools; we need to get the primary schools up here doing technology, French and music and joining in our concerts; we need to rationalize our approach to the media; we need to get on to radio, television and into the educational press. We needed to do something about the appearance of the school, displays in the school; we needed to initiate in-service training about how you talk to parents; we needed to send secretarial staff on training to learn how you talk to people.

The 18-point guide also provided the school with a simple checklist to evaluate their successes or failures. Having set out a three-year and a five-year plan, the school found they had reached most of the three-year objectives within the first 12 months. Similarly, the five-year plan was completed well within three years. 'The acceleration was quite fascinating to me, how once you started to do something you were winning rapidly . . . If you are suddenly in a successful organization, then everybody feels better about it . . .'

Raising money at Garibaldi School

However, Bob was aware that, despite having met so many of the school's objectives, the process had to be continuous and many of the improvements the organization wanted to make to the 'educational package' required resource input which was not available through the normal budget. 'I don't think we were initially looking for extra finance but in the back of my mind I hoped for it. I very much believed the way to stop sponsorship dead was to write a letter to a company saying, "Can you send us some money?" So I had to try something else.'

Bob arranged an appointment with the management of a Derbyshire theme park, 'The American Adventure'. 'I went to ask them for money, not directly but hoping some mutually beneficial idea would materialize. They said they were absolutely stony broke!' The company's reasoning behind their poor performance was directly related to a lack of ticket sales. Bob, with his newly gained marketing expertise, enquired as to how they marketed their product and how many visitors were attracted from the north Nottingham area. Both responses provided Bob with an opportunity of proposing a 'deal'. 'I said, "Well why don't you let us market north Nottinghamshire for you? Provide us with promotionally priced tickets, we will sell them for you and take a cut of the profit." ' The theme park management agreed and within the first three months Garibaldi, utilizing cheap advertising arrangements, negotiated with their local newspaper, had sold over £17,000 worth of tickets. Garibaldi's proceeds were used to purchase a school minibus.

However, the Garibaldi marketing campaign had proved so successful that it came to the notice of a larger competitor of 'The American Adventure' – Alton Towers in Staffordshire. Three businessmen arrived one day at the school and said they wanted to talk to Bob Salisbury about ticket sales. The offer they made was that, if Garibaldi shifted loyalty from 'The American Adventure' to Alton Towers, they would provide the school with a better deal – a better reduction on tickets, support for advertising and a better share in the profits. Bob's question, 'OK, what's in it for you, why us?', elicited the response (which is perhaps the first example of a large corporation recognizing entrepreneurial activity in a school which could have a direct influence on its own operation): 'We've seen what you have been doing and we are just saying why not shift allegiance to us, because we are a better company and together we have got a better future.'

Another of Bob's excursions into the world of business involved making contact with British Thornton, a scientific and educational equipment manufacturer. 'I said to them, "Where do your customers see your equipment?" and they said, "In our brochure or in Manchester at our factory showroom". I then asked, "Well, how many people come to Manchester?" and he said, "None." ' Bob then suggested that the company build showrooms at the school: a modern languages centre, a new science laboratory and a new home economics room, together forming an East Midlands centre where prospective purchasers could see the various products not only displayed but also in use and where the Garibaldi staff would be available to discuss products and show visitors around.

Aware of the resource implications to British Thornton, Bob also suggested that the school would show its commitment to the partnership by putting up half of the refurbishment costs. 'So that is what we did and I claimed the matching funding required from the Greater Nottingham Training and Enterprise Council (TEC, a central government-funded body, one of whose aims is to provide resource input to encourage educational and business partnerships) for our half so it didn't cost us anything! The deal was successful for both parties, British Thornton gained three relatively cheap "product-activity-based" showrooms and Garibaldi not only received the improvements to three of their teaching areas but also a 3% commission on any orders generated. The benefits to the school went even beyond the potential for revenue and school improvements. . . . When you get a group from another school coming to see the products, they come with all sorts of ideas. They wander around the school saying, "Why didn't you do this?" and you say, "I don't know; good idea, we'll do it." '

This involvement with the TEC was enhanced once the new language centre was up and running, by a link made with a company called Applied Language Services. The company now administratively based at Garibaldi, a service offered by the school, provides evening and weekend language courses for business companies, utilizing the facilities of the school. 'The beauty of the partnership is that it is subsidized through the TEC, provides much-needed revenue, uses our facilities during slack periods and it also brings another forty-five or so business people into the school at any one time. Educationally it is a nice link.'

Utilizing the administrative skills available within the school has also provided the opportunity of taking the idea of providing exhibition space to businesses, particularly where they are aiming at the broader educational market. One company, Trent Copyfax, have found that using Garibaldi for exhibitions is not only successful in providing a backdrop for their products but also is administratively effortless for the company, with the school's team taking over the exhibition organization which involves the arrangement of refreshments, the facilities required and even the marketing of the exhibition to other schools.

The effectiveness of the entrepreneurial activity

The culture change at Garibaldi is still under way but Bob and other members of staff point to the projects as concrete evidence of the move from a static hierarchical institution to a fluid system of 'bobbing corks':

The inside and outside of the school just look so much better. We have the French street for realistic and exciting teaching, the new state-of-the-art language laboratories, all the improvements we are making in the technical area rooms and there just isn't the damage any more – not like there used to be. On top of that we have a team of staff looking at equal opportunities – we want more than a written statement. Then there is a possibility of a leisure centre on the site in a joint venture with the community. People and other schools keep coming to see what we are doing or ask me to visit them. There is so much going on I have almost lost track!

Is his enterprise enhancing the growth of entrepreneurial activity within the community itself? Through creativity and hard work he has changed completely the culture and fortunes of the Garibaldi School over a very short period of time. It may be that the new independence given to UK schools since the 1988 Education Act has helped to provide the opportunity for many of the changes that he has introduced, but there is no question, with the range of innovation introduced, that he has shown the ability to enhance imaginatively the resource base of the school.

The pupils

All of the 1000-plus pupils of the school are taught presentation skills, provided with self-confidence building activities, and encouraged to generate ideas which might be beneficial only on an individual basis or in the wider community. An example of this was the national prize won by a group of sixth formers who wrote and presented a plan for schools in the year 2000. The prizes were a financial reward for each team member plus an additional award for the school as a whole.

The innovatory activities of the Garibaldi School have enabled the teaching staff to broaden the pupils' parameters of activity. On the one hand, pupils have far greater contact with industrialists, the community at large, media people and academics; whilst on the other, the number of educational visits has increased, with trips to Stratford-upon-Avon and even European countries now becoming a normal part of the pupils' lives.

'Success breeds success.' This seems to be an important part of the community entrepreneur's role – providing the examples of success for the pupils to emulate, whilst simultaneously heightening their overall expectations. The number of pupils who now look towards further and higher education has increased dramatically; they no longer see problems as being insurmountable and have also developed a pride in their school and community.

The adults

If, as is argued, there is a direct relationship between economic growth and the educational attainment of the population, then the activities at Garibaldi culminating in the enhancement of local adults' basic skills must be assisting the local regeneration; these activities are as diverse as basic literacy skills and German for business.

The activities at Garibaldi have increased the community's confidence in facilitating change by watching an organization transform itself from being previously recognized as 'bad' to one that is now applauded as an organization of the highest quality. People now travel to the school's area rather than avoiding Clipstone.

There is an increasing level of self-esteem amongst many of the adults involved with the school and their expectations for both themselves and their children are changing with an apparent reduction in their acceptance of continuing depression.

State schools in the UK are not profit-making organizations; there are no shareholders to satisfy and this probably encourages much greater generosity in 'sharing' than is generally found in the business entrepreneur. Bob Salisbury spends a great deal of his time talking to people and, as he would put it, sharing his 'vision'. This vision goes far beyond the activities of the school, just one example being his plans for a shared leisure centre on the school campus.

He is also very concerned that other schools should benefit from his successes, not only in the gained expertise he can pass on at head teacher Development Days, but also in practical terms. For example, one school in London has benefited from Bob's contacts in Alton Towers and now has a similar deal to Garibaldi based on ticket sales in the West London area.

These networks are providing the pupils with tremendous benefits, such as jobs when leaving school, work experience during their school career and the input of practitioners to their classroom work. It could also be suggested that many of the projects initiated by Bob, which would not have got off the ground without his extensive networking, have provided the local community with an enhanced feeling of self-confidence and thrusting enterprise. These might include the development of the crèche at the school, the EuroCentre, the proposed joint leisure centre, the regeneration of the decaying school building, the increasing traffic of the business community to the school and the desire by parents to send their children to a community they would have once avoided when selecting the best education for their children.

12

A NEW ROLE FOR THE THIRD SECTOR

Usha Prashar

Let me begin by defining the kind of third sector I am interested in. I am talking about a third sector which will enable participation, involvement and provide a voice for local people to ensure that they have a stake in society. The third sector should be accountable, able to reflect priorities and meet needs: it should connect people, act as a glue between constituent communities, help mediate conflicts and help develop shared values.

We have to remember that the community-based approach goes back a long way, and its achievements are numerous. These can best be seen in the tasks which have been completed and groups that have been helped. For example, green belts have been preserved, people from different ethnic backgrounds have found a place to meet and talk, groups have been made aware of their entitlements, community arts groups have been established. But the 'community movement' has not fully succeeded in fostering a more embracing sense of community or providing training in democratic citizenship or enabling people to formulate a vision of the future which they would work to bring about in fellowship with their neighbours.

In my view the 'community movement' has not fully succeeded mainly due to the context and the environment within which it has been operating. Its full potential has neither been recognized nor enabled to be released. It is true that community initiatives depend on people themselves but it is equally true to say that our current political processes do not do justice to the rich variety and potential of the third sector. Politicians implement their policies from top down and do not harness energies on the ground. What we need are processes which will encourage participation, processes which will shift us away from representative democracy to a participatory mode of democracy. We need arrangements which will ensure a centre stage for the third sector, which in turn will involve people and give them a sense of involvement, purpose and pride in society.

Now, for their own divergent reasons, the political parties are turning to communities or becoming 'community minded'. Questions are being asked about how to revive 'community spirit' and encourage more responsible citizens. My contention is that we have not lost the community spirit but that it has not been harnessed constructively. It is now clear that one theme which is likely to dominate the debate into the millennium is the importance of the community and civil life, and the organizations that give expression to people's sense of responsibility. However, we have to recognize that the current political interest in the third sector is mainly due to political parties' interest in promoting social cohesion and social stability. This contains the danger that the third sector will be used for short-term gains.

While it is true that the third sector's true potential can, to a large extent, only be harnessed by a congenial political and economic framework, it is equally important that the third sector does things for itself and begins to consider long-term issues. There are some long-term issues which should underpin the current interest in the role of the third sector if we are to rebuild sustainable communities and refocus government for the third millennium. This has implications for the third sector, political parties and government.

First of all we have to be clear why we need to encourage and enable the third sector to play an important role. We also have to be clear about the limitations and the potential of the third sector and how we need to facilitate a central role for the sector.

It is essential to dispel the traditional view of the third sector as Lady Bountiful, doing good unto others, or viewed with suspicion as usurping the role of the state or as a safety net. Instead, it has to be seen as a force which will play a significant role in transforming the way people think, work and participate in society. It is for the third sector to make a strong case to convince others of its potential and the role it can play; this means marshalling arguments more clearly, strongly and convincingly. In my view, if the third sector is to be instrumental in rebuilding communities then it has to be valued for its intrinsic worth and not just as a cost-effective alternative.

First, it needs to be shown clearly that it is a vehicle which fosters and encourages self-reliance and has the ability to identify and provide public services appropriately and flexibly. Second, it encourages participation and a sense of involvement through which people begin to feel that they not only have a stake in society but also an ability to influence events. Third, it is a fertile ground for innovation, doing things differently and giving opportunities to social entrepreneurs. Fourth, third-sector organizations are value-based organizations which encourage responsibility, autonomy, self-realization, a sense of give and take, and encourage the public good and mutual benefit.

This, of course, puts a great responsibility on the third sector and the way it operates. It has to be transparent, accountable and aspire to high moral and ethical standards where means as well as ends are important. It has to be seen not just as an add-on 'charity' but as a force for good – public good, with the main purpose of serving and enabling participation and representation. It can be a forum for conflict resolution, for enabling cohesiveness and consensus through dialogue while respecting differences.

The government or the state, on the other hand, has to enable a congenial environment or framework which promotes, enables and harnesses the positive aspects of the third sector. This, of course, means refocusing government in providing an appropriate formal apparatus of legal, fiscal arrangements and statutory services which form the structure of law and order, social cohesion and service. We need a style of government which is not just 'top down' but creates a framework for initiative and 'bottom up' approaches.

We need to debate what kind of legal and fiscal conditions we need to create a new role for the third sector, what kind of local government and local democracy we need and what kind of relationship between government, political processes and the third sector. We need this relationship to be dynamic – a two-way relationship which is responsive, receptive, encourages the third sector to innovate, agitate, irritate and interrogate so that our democracy remains vibrant and responsive. Within the overarching framework would lie a large number of diverse organizations which people set up or join of their own free will in order to meet their own and other people's needs and to express their values and concerns as they see them. This would create a healthy democracy, which would encourage initiative, responsibility and appropriate channels for building consensus, resolving conflicts and would provide a springboard for economic prosperity and health of society at large.

All of this is not without dilemmas. There are, of course, limitations, but to date we have not fully realized the potential of the third sector and we should not paralyse ourselves by just debating dilemmas but take action where it is possible. A good place to start would be to begin by identifying the current constraints which inhibit community action and what steps can be taken to remove these. Let us begin by building upon the experiences and successes of the 'community movement' to date.

13

FUNDING COMMUNITY DEVELOPMENT TRUSTS

People-led regeneration

The best route to sustainable community regeneration is to connect investment in economic, physical and social capital. The key to this is the involvement of local people. The creation of Community Development Trusts
would provide an institutional base for regeneration led by local people.

A new National Community Regeneration Agency (NCRA) should be set
up to support the establishment of local regeneration initiatives and audit
the work of local Trusts.

Once the NCRA is satisfied that communities have demonstrated willingness and capacity to share responsibility for regeneration, funding would be
allocated to newly designated Community Development Trusts.

Local groups and individuals would be able to approach the Trust with
ideas for projects to be funded. The Trust would be co-ordinated by a locally
elected board and would be established as a non-profit distributing charity.

It would be the task of the Trust to develop working links with the
authority, local employers and training agencies and to reflect the local
regeneration priorities.

The Trust's mission would be to develop the social wealth, quality of life
and reputation of the area, reconnecting the community to mainstream
education, training and job opportunities.

Trusts should focus on long-term sustainability by developing new funding sources and contracts. Their work could support emerging intermediate
labour markets and community development banks.

Extract from the Borrie Commission on Social Justice, p.331.

COMMUNITY – THE ECONOMIC AND ENVIRONMENTAL BUILDING BLOCKS

*Self-confident people and neighbourhoods can only be sustained
if the economic infrastructure is soundly based.
So it is important to ask what contribution the
third and private sectors can make to that infrastructure.*

14

WORK

Charles Handy

I admire Howard Gardner who is based in Boston. He came up with the idea of multiple intelligences, and identified seven forms; the technical terms he used are not important here. I have myself identified nine or ten forms: let me briefly describe a few of them.

The first is what I call mastermind intelligence – people who know a lot of things; they're pretty boring people, because they insist on telling them to you. Then there's what you might call logical, analytical, intelligence – people who can reason. There is also linguistic intelligence – people who can actually use language, their own language or many other languages. Now, these are not necessarily connected. I have a friend who talks eight languages fluently but his wife told me he talks nonsense in all of them!

These three intelligences are the ones we concentrate on in our schools these days. Schools are concerned with factual intelligence, ability to read and ability to write it all down in one language or another. But there are many more kinds. There is pattern intelligence. Artists have the ability to see patterns and links, but so do entrepreneurs: they can see gaps in markets that nobody else can, or opportunities in society that nobody else can. The trouble is that this intelligence is not necessarily connected with the other three. People who have it often do very badly at school and think they're failures. Of course, the worst thing that an entrepreneur needs to think is that he or she is a failure.

There is also musical intelligence. This doesn't just entail playing the clarinet very well. Members of pop groups – who don't seem to be able to get into university – have it: they go off and tour the world and have great fun.

Then there is physical or sporting intelligence. Our great sports stars have great skill and great ability and they can be very successful, and they make lots of friends.

We also have practical intelligence, what I call common sense – would that it were more common. This doesn't get graded at school either; we often call it being 'streetwise'. Then there is intuitive intelligence which knows instinctively what's right and what's wrong. I have great logical intelligence; my wife has great intuitive intelligence. So I win all the arguments and she says 'Well you're wrong.'

Lastly, there is inter-personal intelligence. This is the ability to get other people to do the things that you would like them to do and they were wanting to do; call it leadership or management, if you like. It is not necessarily correlated with any of the others. Somebody came to my business who had a double first in chemistry and a first in history. We said 'It's very doubtful that you will make a manager', because such intelligences are often not correlated.

Now, if you share my faith that every single person has at least one, and maybe two and possibly three, of these intelligences in a world where intelligence and know-how of all sorts are the way to prosperity, comfort and happiness, you can see the possibilities. If only we can find a way to help people identify which intelligence they have and how to use it to the benefit of others – that's the problem.

Of course, it should be the job of our schools to solve this problem but, as education takes place in all sorts of other places, it gets answered, if at all, elsewhere. All I learnt in school was that every problem in the world had already been solved: it was just that I didn't know the answer, the teacher did. That totally incapacitated me for life in the modern world, because every time I had a problem, I ran for help to an expert. Eventually my boss said: 'You have no initiative, you will never make a leader, you couldn't talk the hind leg off a donkey if you knew what a donkey was.'

Take the virtual library. People think they need places to go to, which are central like the library. But a few months ago, very sadly, the central library in Norwich burnt down and the librarian who lives in our village in Norfolk was heartbroken. I saw him recently and he was a man reborn: he'd got all the insurance money and his prime site in the centre of Norwich. So, he had the choice, either to rebuild the central library or to use the money on technology instead. If he did this, he could put a room, as a library, in every hamlet and every village in Norfolk. These rooms would connect with a central resource, not necessarily in the centre of Norwich, and with all the libraries around the world through the Internet. So everybody could walk in to that global library and have all the information in the world right there in their village. He said to me: 'Do you know what the most thumbed book in the central library in Norwich is? It's the *Guide to the Electrician's Regulations for the Common Market*. Because people don't go to libraries any more so much to borrow books on romance and so on: they go there because there's a source of information that they need for work when they are independent.'

In my world half the workforce is inevitably going to be outside of an organization. So, where do they get their skills and information from? They go to the library. So, we need a library in every community; and we can do it. 'Except there's one thing,' my librarian said. 'We've got this interesting decision.' I know what he'll do; he'll rebuild the central library because the politicians won't believe the other alternative and his staff won't want it. Too many old habits get in the way of possibilities for the future.

In future, individuals are going to have to be more responsible for their lives and for their work. But before they're grown up, young people need godparents: they need help to grow up. So what we need in communities are 'godparent groups'. Now who can they be?

First of all, I believe, godparents can be found in the work organizations, the businesses that already exist. You only learn to work at work and with workers: you don't learn to work at school. I believe there could be people who were at work, retired people, who would like to give something back to the community; and there should be opportunities for them to do that, by being godparents. I'm trying to persuade the trade union movement that this is their opportunity and I had this wonderful conversation with a member of the TUC who said to me: 'We have this very interesting decision to take in the trade union movement. Will we continue to represent the rump of the employed labour force in the old industries and businesses of Britain or will we take on the challenge of the new workforce?' 'Oh, indeed,' I said, 'what's the new workforce?' 'Well,' he said, 'all these people outside the organization, the independents, part-timers, the temporaries who need all the help we can give them.' 'Wonderful,' I said. 'Yes,' he said. 'There's no doubt what we shall decide. We will continue to represent the rump labour force of the old industries and services of Britain.'

Yet there is a marvellous opportunity here for the people who run those little libraries, as well as a wonderful opportunity for our schools. Should we put our libraries there or, maybe, we could put the libraries into the churches. Wouldn't that be exciting, too, because somebody's got to use these buildings.

Then I want to move our benefit system to a citizen's income. I want to take all those mortgage reliefs that shouldn't exist and all those pension funds and all those other taxes and pensions and benefits, and wrap them all up into a citizen's income which is given to everybody, regardless of age, regardless of status, regardless of nationality or whether in work or out of work. It won't be very much to start with: it might only be £25 to £30 a week to everybody. You can't live on that. But five citizen's incomes added together could just about support a household. So, I want to use economics to push people back into kinship groups. I don't want to say families, because it might not be a conventional family, but it will huddle people together instead of pushing them into lonely little rooms.

The world will become more and more high-tech – you can't avoid it. You will have a personal telephone and you will have a personal telephone number and will go shopping by TV in due course. And, the more high-tech you get, the more high-touch you want. You'll do it in blocks. At the moment, you have high-tech and high-touch altogether when you go to work. In future, you'll have high-tech one day and high-touch the next. And that will make a convivial society, I suspect.

We need to have places for the high-touch and one of them should be the home. I have hopes of the third age. These are the people who will now be leaving the organizations. They'll be worn out, tired, overpaid but fat, bald and too expensive, in their early fifties. Yet, they will still want to contribute to society and there's going to be lots of things for them to do. Maybe their motivations will have changed by then: they will no longer need to accumulate endless possessions but, perhaps, wish to give something back because there's no use being rich in the graveyard!

I believe that we will redefine work to mean not just work for money but work in the home, looking after people, cooking and so on, which women know is work. But when more men start to do it, they will make it respectable: that will be good news. Let's call it 'gift work' in the community and, above all, perhaps, 'study work'. Studying is work and it will be regarded as such as more adults do it. And so everybody will be able to say they're working. Further, everybody will be able to say they're working with other people. My daughter said to me, 'Dad, I like work but I don't want to work for anybody. I just want to work with people.' That's going to be much more possible in this day and age.

So these are the possibilities. If you think it won't happen, I'd just like you to remember two names, which you may know.

Abe Maslow[1], an American psychologist, had a hierarchy of needs. He said you start off with just being physically safe; then having enough money to keep warm and well fed; then having some kind of social identity; and eventually you get to the fifth level need: self-fulfilment or self-actualization. So, when you've got enough money and all the rest of it, then you can strive for self-fulfilment. When I studied that it seemed to make selfishness too respectable. Just at the end of his life, he thought so too. In the preface to his last book he wrote: 'Maybe there's a sixth need beyond self-fulfilment which is perhaps idealization.'

I would say that the only purpose that really satisfies is a purpose beyond oneself. What is exciting is that our society is rich: most people in Britain are rich beyond all thinking of my parents. So, we are now ready to have a purpose beyond our self. I find people itching for this. Thus, politicians who preach greed and economic growth are missing an opportunity. They do not see that people want to have a purpose beyond themselves.

If you say: 'Well, let's hope somebody gives us that leadership,' I say: 'Remember Roland Hill.' He's my wife's ancestor. He was the man who did the penny post, you'll know that. You will probably also know that in the 1830s it cost 1s 6d to send a letter from London to Edinburgh because you priced the letter according to the distance it travelled, and the recipient had to pay. So you had to be very sure that you wanted my letter before I wrote it. As a result, fewer people wrote letters and the price went up, of course. So, Roland Hill said: 'Wouldn't it be sensible to turn it upside down and charge a penny for every letter however far it went?' Thus, you could purchase the price of the letter before it went, so you paid for a stamp which you could stick on the letter.

Roland Hill's brother invented the perforated strip so you could tear it off quickly – a good family business there. Of course nobody believed him, and the Post Office said: 'That's silly, we'll lose so much money.' The government said: 'Don't be silly, we've got a good system, why spoil it?' But, anyway, after ten years of badgering and complaining and leading petitions and all the rest of it, it did change. Parliament changed it. Within five years the Post Office was rolling in money. Within ten years 55 countries had adopted it.

For the first time people had learned to read and write because there was a point to it. Because you could actually write to your son who had left for London and you'd never heard of him again and he couldn't travel back. Roland Hill changed the literacy habits of a country; he totally changed the aspirations of a nation. Wasn't that exciting? But the really interesting thing about Roland Hill was that when he did all this, he had given up teaching in despair and had joined the South Australia Company in the Strand as a clerk. Changing the postal system was literally none of his business. But he thought it would be 'a good idea'. So he did it and he changed the world. So, if you think you're going to wait for somebody in Westminster or somebody in the Birmingham City Council to do it all for you now, just remember Roland Hill. We can all change the world, and now's the time.

Notes and references

1. Maslow, A. (1994) *The Further Reaches of Human Nature*. Harmondsworth: Penguin.

15

THE ECONOMY OF THE THIRD SECTOR

Ian Morrison

A serious discussion about the economy and value of the third sector risks offending the purists at two opposite ends of the spectrum. Some in the third sector would argue that organizations within the sector should not be evaluated in economic terms; rather, they should be valued for the social benefit which they provide. At the other end of the spectrum there are those who would argue that economic value is concerned primarily with manufacturing and wealth creation. Happily this is not the complete picture; the notion of the social economy, and the way in which social and economic gain are interlinked, have gained considerable ground in recent times, and the social economy has become a subject of increased importance.

Nevertheless there is still little public appreciation of the way in which the third sector contributes to the economic well-being of society. This chapter suggests that the third sector role is vital and provides some simple indicators of the way in which a new perspective of the sector's value might be developed and publicly recognized.

The basis on which the sector is valued is generally conceived in rather vague and nebulous ways. Commonly any estimate of the value of the third sector is based upon the perceived social value of its functions. The altruism of voluntary activity is acknowledged; similarly 'self-help' is usually regarded as a 'good thing'. Obviously this recognition of the contribution made to the social and moral fabric of the community is vital, though frequently underplayed. The third sector itself must take some responsibility for this, for it has all too often failed to recognize its own worth and, in consequence, promote itself effectively to the public and private sectors.

In particular, the third sector has failed to emphasize that it plays a major role in the economic arrangements of communities. Its social worth may be recognized but scant attention or regard has been given to the indispensable contribution which it makes to the economy. The prevailing search for 'value for money', 'additionality', etc. within present economic thinking provides opportunities which have not yet been fully exploited by the third sector as a means of establishing the sector's value.

At the same time, the increasing movement towards 'partnership' within public sector provision suggests that there is a change in the current climate. While 'partnership' has become commonplace in the vocabulary of decision-makers of all political persuasions, there is both an opportunity and a threat. The threat is that, unless the sector is able to establish equality as a basis for partnership, the current trend will simply be a mechanism for continuing patronage of the sector. Voluntary organizations will remain as supplicants at the tables of the decision-makers, constrained by the need to achieve funding for their work. The opportunities will only be realized if the sector is able to establish that it brings to the table a range of unique and distinct contributions and functions to the economic as well as the social fabric of community life.

Equality in partnership will not be achieved simply by asserting that it should exist. This could merely lead to superficial behavioural changes, a form of tokenism, in which no more than lip service is paid by way of acknowledgement of the third sector's contribution. Any real engagement in, or influence upon, decision-making will continue to be no more than marginal.

If equality in the partnerships between the three sectors is to be achieved, then attitudinal changes are also essential. These attitudinal shifts will only occur as a consequence of increased understanding, knowledge and a concomitant recognition of the value of each partner. The third sector is much more financially powerful than is supposed; this power is scarcely recognized, and therefore little used. Considerable effort is needed to rectify this. Although there is already a range of work which would form the basis of a very strong case, it is only relatively recently that such arguments are beginning to be put. This need for a re-evaluation of the sector and its economic importance is crucial, otherwise it is likely that all that will be achieved is the perpetuation of the situation in which the sector is consulted only up to the point at which financial priorities are determined.

Encouraging support for a re-evaluation of the economic role of the third sector comes from Sir Dennis Landau, Chairman of Unity Trust Bank. He said: 'British economic thinking is imprisoned by the distinction between the public and private sectors. I happen to be convinced there is a tremendous need for a recognition of this third sector.'

There are already a number of statistics which prove that the economic force of the third sector has been significantly underestimated. For example, in part justification of his view, according to Sir Dennis, the third sector accounts for perhaps 10% of the GDP, whilst manufacturing has shrunk to 19% of GDP. Other evidence is available to support such a stance.

For example: in work undertaken by the National Council of Voluntary Organizations (NCVO) it was estimated that the labour force of the voluntary sector in this country is approximately half a million people, which is larger than the agricultural industry. Other work undertaken by the John Hopkins University, USA, and work in the UK by Kent University, confirm that as many as one in twenty jobs worldwide occur within not-for-profit organizations. Yet despite these kinds of figures there is little recognition of the sector as a major employer.

Other available figures begin to highlight the economic importance of the sector. In work carried out by the Community Development Foundation (CDF) it was shown that five years ago voluntary workers/carers were saving the social services of this country some £25bn. The more recent changes in provision of services and the delivery of community care are likely to have dramatically increased this figure. CDF further predict that the social economy will grow from 10% to 30% in the next ten years.

Prompted by the evidence of this and other work carried out on a wider scale, a more modest pilot piece of work was undertaken in Birmingham by the Birmingham Voluntary Service Council (BVSC). The work aimed in a fairly simple way to look at a range of economic factors in relation to voluntary and charitable organizations within the city. The work was limited and the authors suggest some caution in relation to the figures and advise that the finding should be regarded as indicative rather than definitive. Nevertheless the work points to a number of significant features in the economic profile of organizations and the voluntary sector in the city. Some of the findings are cited here as a means of illustrating the usefulness of investigation of this kind in developing a sound case for the sector locally.

In a sample of 200 organizations (some estimates suggest that there are well over two thousand organizations in the city) the annual cash turnover of those organizations was in excess of £37m. National estimates suggest that the turnover of voluntary and charitable organizations is in the region of £15bn.

In the Birmingham sample 19.4% of the funding came from local authority. 26% of funding came from central government sources, although with the demise of the Urban Programme and the cutbacks signified by the creation of the Single Regeneration Budget this figure is likely to diminish considerably.

49% of voluntary sector funding was self-generated by organizations through their own efforts. From a public sector point of view this has to be seen as extremely good value for money. The leverage value of local authority money in the city can be expressed as follows: for every £1 of local authority money invested in the voluntary sector a further £4.09 is gained from all other sources.

Other figures within the work point to the value of the human resources. By very conservative estimates, from the sample of 200 organizations including volunteers, the value of the labour used in one year totalled in excess of £10m. Evidence shows that the paid and unpaid workforce possess, on average, significantly higher than the average educational and vocational qualifications than are likely to be found elsewhere.

Further it is established that, 'Without the opportunity that voluntary activity presents to so many, the knowledge, skill, and frequently costly training which they possess would be wasted for lack of any outlet. In economic terms this has to be seen as a waste of a valuable asset.'

The opportunity to utilize existing skills is given added weight by consideration of people who are able to maintain or develop skills which are subsequently used in the private or public sectors. There are, for example, an increasing number of graduates who are undertaking voluntary work as a means of enhancing job prospects. Because of the usually more flexible working arrangements of the sector, the opportunities the sector provides for women who may subsequently wish to return to paid work is of great value.

The role of the sector as a means by which skill and time are invested by individuals is further highlighted in another section of the report which looked at the languages used in the organizations surveyed. It is argued that there are almost negligible opportunities outside the voluntary sector for those who use a mother tongue other than English to become engaged at an organizational level in civic, social and economic affairs. Apart from the disempowerment and alienation of individuals this can cause, it also represents a loss of talent and ability directed towards the economic and social well-being of the community at large.

Investment is a major issue in any economic overview. As we have already outlined, third-sector contributions to the economy can be the means by which local people may invest in their own neighbourhood. That investment may take many forms: knowledge, skills expertise, time and even money. On a wider scale such investment is not confined to local neighbourhoods. Work carried out in the Birmingham study shows that significant levels of voluntary activity occur at city, regional, national and international levels.

At some stage, cash becomes a fact of life, and of course financial investment is a crucial further element. It is one not usually seen as being within the province of the third sector. To a large degree this may be true if one considers the role of the sector as a potential investor. On the other hand, the third sector is increasingly becoming a means by which invest-ment may be attracted and made within an area. For example, there is considerable money available through European funding regimes which can only be accessed by local and voluntary organizations. The new purchaser/ provider relationships being established across public sector finance lends added weight to this view. Voluntary and charitable organizations, particu-larly in the potentially less profitable rural areas, become the focus of investment and contribute to the net disposable income circulating within the area.

There are other factors around investment to which the third sector can make a particular contribution. The ability to target investment is vital and the third sector is frequently 'needs led'. It is acknowledged to have a more flexible approach which allows for the targeting of investment to meet specific needs with greater accuracy. It is not always the large-scale investment programmes that in the longer term prove to be the most valuable. Recent movements towards local partnerships in investment programmes are perhaps the beginning of a recognition of the value of the third sector in this respect.

There are other less tangible benefits derived from third-sector activity which represent a mixture of social and economic gain. Their social signific-ance is more immediately obvious and much more clearly understood. Nevertheless their economic value, though relatively unrecognized, is of considerable worth. In Section 1 of this book Bob Tyrell points out the correlation between individuals' engagement in community and the incid-ence of crime. He argues that there is convincing evidence to support the view that a fall in the involvement in community life is accompanied by an increase in criminal activity. The connections between such evidence and a discussion of economic activity may appear less obvious than the clear social implications, but it has relevance here in a number of important ways.

First, there is the issue of cost. Criminal activity has a high financial, as well as social, cost. The cost of maintaining crime prevention and detection services and all the apparatus of judicial and penal processes is massively increasing. At a time when public sector finance continues to escalate alarmingly, anything which can contribute to a halt in such increases must be seen to have a high economic value.

Second, wealth-creating activities do not take place 'in vacuo'. Manufac-turing and private-sector activity needs to take place within a favourable social context. The demographic evidence contained in the most recent census figures, which highlight the ways in which some of the most disadvantaged and vulnerable groups in our society continue to be alien-ated, has a bearing upon economic regeneration in the longer term. Main-taining and improving the social fabric of society are just as important a feature of economic activity. For, without them, the conditions necessary for successful entrepreneurial activity will not be there and economic success will at best be severely constrained and at worst will simply not take place. Put more simply, programmes of investment are unlikely to prove attractive in areas where there are deep social problems and dissatisfaction with the consequent high levels of criminality.

I have emphasized the importance of the third sector as a force in the economy and suggested that, even on the basis of some very simple analysis, there are grounds to argue for an increased recognition of this role. The intention is not to argue for the primacy of one sector or another but to highlight the interdependence between activity in the public, private and third sectors. In a mixed economy such as ours it is only by working together, with a mutual respect for the contribution to be made by each, that any real and long-term gains will be made. This means that the third sector has to be drawn increasingly into decision-making, in the setting of priorities and the development of plans for economic progress in the future. Partnership has to be seen to operate on the basis of the equality of the partners. There is no complete panacea but we can at least begin to seek solutions together.

16

ENTERPRISING BUSINESS

Karin Jacobson

The office can indeed be as empty and underutilized as the school. I'd like to show how it can be fulfilled with an outline of some 'software' development, to enable shopping centre management to 'do their bit' to enhance their community.

DUSCO acts as asset manager to property investment groups. With them, it acquires and owns large retail centres. Our first major UK investment was in the centre of Nottingham; our second investment is in Birmingham where DUSCO has acquired the Gracechurch Shopping Centre in Sutton Coldfield.

To understand our global and local approach in this area, the following speech made by our Chairman, Dik Dusseldorp, invites us to step back in time.

Tracing the evolution of the seasonal meeting places of the pre-agricultural people shows that in the post-nomadic period these meeting places simply became more permanent, and bigger. More and more people stayed the year round. You could ask the question: Why did they meet in the first place?

I venture to guess that their needs and desires were basically the same as ours today: social interaction, entertainment, the exchange of ideas, goods, gossip and genes. The movement of people changed from 'all over the place' to a movement towards one centre or another in search of convenience, which could only be paid for with work. With permanent settlement came permanent work. The work ethic was born: work or perish.

Not until the arrival of the mass-produced motor car, did the by then crowded centres find new space for expansion. Suburbs now surrounded all major centres of population, which, in time, led to the emergence of shopping centres. These shopping centres had only one aim – to facilitate efficient and convenient shopping. In that, they succeeded.

Unintentionally, they also succeeded in tearing apart the social fabric of the many inner cities so carefully woven over long periods of time; they also separated workers from their jobs. The segregation of mutually supportive functions of the modern meeting places, the urban neighbourhoods from which our cities are constructed, proved very damaging. The consequences are there for all to see: shopping centres in the suburbs and ghettos in the city, and the emergence of an increasingly militant underclass.

Before asking the obvious question: What to do about it?, I first would like to draw on expert economic opinion for additional insights into the broader framework of forces at work in this context. Dr Thurow, Dean at MIT School of Management, in a speech given at the National Retail Federation convention held recently in the United States, posed the question: 'What were the factors that made companies and countries rich in the past?' History would tell you there were four factors, he said.

First, more natural resources, second more capital, third better technology, and fourth, better skills than your competitor. These, combined with reasonable management, was what led to economic success.

How did Britain happen to be the world's wealthiest country in the nineteenth century? By inventing the spinning jenny, perfecting the steam engine, inventing the steel furnace and being lucky enough to have the most accessible coal deposits on earth. The coal deposits fired the steel furnaces, made steam for the engines that powered the spinning jenny and with textiles, steam ships and steam trains, the British could conquer the world.

History also explains how the United States caught up with Great Britain around 1900, passed it and became the world's wealthiest country in the twentieth century. The United States was lucky enough to have more natural resources per capita than any other country on the face of the globe and America put that vast inheritance of natural resources to work by introducing mass universal education and thus overtook the world in time.

So much for the past. So what competitive advantage do we have in the twenty-first century? Natural resources are buyable; capital is borrowable, and product technology is copiable. So, no advantage from these sources.

Dr Thurow sees only one dominant area left: process technology. The heart of process technology is the skills of one's workforce. Our common ground is the importance of skill formation. Dr Thurow's emphasis is on the creation of wealth – ours is to prevent the waste of underskilled workers, which in the end adds up to the same thing.

In Australia in 1989, we responded to this analysis by developing our first student-school-to-work transitional programme which sought to integrate the acquisition of core skills, social skills, and work skills, for youth not destined for higher education. We call it TRAC, which acts as a brand name; it could stand for Trust, Respect And Commitment.

It is important to explain this programme in some detail, for better understanding; not for what should be done but for what is being done. We have developed a partnership between local government, industries, schools and colleges. The learning centre, an off-site location, is situated within the shopping centre, perhaps in an empty basement or underutilized set of offices.

Just as John Rennie described how a community school can profit education and inject life into the neighbourhood, so also the shopping centre can become the dynamo which drives development and provides hands-on, meaningful, work-based education.

In our TRAC Programme, students who visit from school or college are trained in the converted office within the shopping centre in personal development skills. They are required to demonstrate specific workplace competencies, before being linked with mentors who provide further guidance and on-the-job training. Students acquire and demonstrate good workplace skills through work-based learning and competency-based instruction. They gain valuable work experience, learn about career options and understand the connection between achievement and economic self-sufficiency.

The students tell us what motivates them: off-site location; self-paced learning; caring teachers; and access to jobs. In short, TRAC incorporates industry skills' standards into students' education, preparing them better for jobs. We believe that we have found a workable partnership model for achieving measurable results for all concerned and replicable almost anywhere by reallocating existing local resources.

So much for the learning part. We strongly believe, however, that learning and motivation are like Siamese twins: one goes nowhere without the other. We have therefore also developed a competition called the TRAC Challenge, a skill competition amongst employees in the retail/service industry, in the shopping centre. Retail employees compete against each other to recognized industry standards. These events create a lot of interest in participating centres, enhancing skills and morale among the competitors and their employers. They also help to recruit mentors and work placements for our student programmes.

Whilst the learning culture will be a determining factor in the future competitive advantage between one shopping centre and another, other initiatives will also be needed. As centre owners and managers, we know that there is not much you can do about the merchandise or its display. But what we and only we can do is to put meaning into the title community centre. It is widely used, but generally with as much hot air as a balloon.

We should try to incorporate in our centres what we have destroyed in the inner cities – its good business, its good community. So, we are revamping the antiquated arrangements for marketing and promotion between tenants and owners. We no longer see tenants as our principal customers. We seek to bring customers to their door for servicing.

We are experimenting with other innovative approaches from Centre Management. For example, why not place within the shopping centres: day-care centres, for employees only; literacy centres, providing English as a second language; and employee skill development programmes?

The list is as endless as employers, customers and competitors may require; it is simply a question of how creative you can get. Fostering only some of these activities attracts community goodwill totally out of proportion to the efforts required. So does the notion of shopping centres, shops and businesses getting together to create a better environment in the centre of town. It is good for mutual business.

The cost? Try seriously to cost staff turnover, customer dissatisfaction and weak community for a change. Opportunities for failure and success are going to be greater than ever. Only good leadership of a skilled, flexible and well-motivated workforce can hope to succeed. The absence of these ingredients, however, is a sure ticket to oblivion and the breakdown not just of city centres but of the quality of life in the surrounding urban villages.

17

BUSINESS AND THE COMMUNITY

David Grayson

If more of the solutions to the problems that British society faces must be found at a local, community level, several things follow. For example, the decentralization of power is not just about transferring responsibilities from government to local councils, but also further down still, from local councils to community organizations and Development Trusts and settlements. Thus, government and local authority regeneration strategy should only go ahead in the future where there is genuine community input.

This process will require new funding mechanisms for community development. See, for instance, the Bronx local council in New York, which collaborated with utility companies on a regeneration strategy and financed their part of the strategy by selling on the future *increase* in tax revenues which the regeneration will produce, to institutional investors; or the deal done in Massachusetts several years ago between the State legislature and the insurance industry which led to the State Government withdrawing proposals for further taxes on the insurance industry, and the industry making a voluntary contribution to finance the establishment of the Community Finance Development Corporation to provide long-term financing for community development agencies.

Business in the Community has taken a modest initiative towards new funding mechanisms with the launch of the Local Initiative Fund to provide loans for community enterprise. If the pilot stage is successful, the objective is to try and persuade the Treasury to give a tax break, perhaps a community version of a PEP or a TESSA account, to encourage private investors to invest in community regeneration.

If there is to be a serious expansion of community-based development it also requires an investment in capacity building and ongoing training and support for the activists and staff of community development organizations. Many of these are 'community entrepreneurs'. How do we 'clone' the successful community entrepreneurs who are now operating in many of the toughest areas of the UK – and maximize their impact? Part at least of that answer lies in the business world.

Established companies have a vested interest in a more cohesive society – just as society has a vested interest in more internationally competitive business – because it is from such business that we generate the wherewithal to help to pay for schools, hospitals and other community services.

We do not want business to become government or a social organization; we do not want government to become a business; we do not want community organizations to become government or business. There are, however, skills and strengths from each sector which can help – and, put together, they can be a powerful combination.

There are already some excellent individual examples of companies giving assistance. More than one thousand voluntary sector managers, for example, have already been through a custom-designed training programme which IBM has put together and run. Bill Castell, the Chief Executive of Amersham International, has personally mentored John Morgan, a community entrepreneur on the Penrhys Estate in South Wales.

The regional brewers Vaux have adopted the Ford and Pennywell Community Advice Centre in Sunderland – and Vaux Breweries' MD, Frank Nicholson, is co-chair with a local community activist, of the Pride of Pennywell campaign, to recreate a sense of community pride and solidarity in a part of Sunderland hard hit by shipbuilding closures and unemployment.

Several hundred professional firms, ranging from accountants and architects to engineers and quantity surveyors, have committed some of their time and expertise for free through organizations like Business in the Community's Professional Firms Groups, inspired by Christopher Jonas of Drivers Jonas. Procter & Gamble on Tyneside have designed training courses on total quality management for head teachers confronted with implementing major educational reforms, and for small-business support organizations operating in areas of high unemployment.

Granada Television have run the Granada Community Challenge involving five major North West employers each recruiting a team of volunteers to tackle an Anneka Rice-type community challenge from a neighbourhood of high social deprivation. And in turn, community organizations have been 'wising up' to the most effective utilization of corporate support.

On a recent tour of the London Lighthouse (the pioneering centre for those living with AIDS), it was noticeable that the Lighthouse was not looking for general volunteers from the big companies on the tour, but for very specific expertise in the form of employees who could mentor the twenty-plus members of the Lighthouse management team and help to develop their managerial capacities.

It makes long-term, business sense for companies to use some of their five Ps: people, premises, product, profits and their power to help community entrepreneurs. Corporate support for Centrepoint, the charity working with the young homeless, illustrates the range of ways in which business can help:

- MEPC sponsored Centrepoint's 25th Anniversary. This included new stationery, annual report, events, and most significantly, the Silver Ball. Once the sponsorship was secured, staff began to get involved with the charity, as one of the senior directors was a Friday night volunteer at Off the Street shelter, and his staff were impressed with his commitment.

- In late summer 1993 LASMO were revamping their corporate giving programme. Until then involvement in the community had been very conservative, with an overall budget being distributed to as many charities as possible. The company realized, however, that this meant that little impact was made for any one charity. So they decided to look for a youth/child charity with a London project. They wanted the company to match donations raised by staff, aiming for a total of £94,000 and also get staff involved in the project. They chose Centrepoint, and the project was to set up a Sunday Club at the Berwick Street Shelter. Volunteers prepare a simple lunch for young people, and then set up recreational activities for them.
- Reuters London staff committee wanted to do something to help. Centrepoint suggested a garden project at our hostel in Kings Cross, and Reuters found a team of volunteers. Intake Hostel is now the proud owner of a small, but beautiful garden.
- Goldman Sachs are in the process of establishing a Goldman Sachs in the Community Programme, to complement the donations they give to charities. The aim of the programme is to get staff to become volunteers for charity. Some have already become business advisers for the PYBT and now GS are working with Centrepoint. Ideas for volunteering include:
  (a) emergency foreign language volunteers: a database of GS people who can be called up at work or home to communicate with young people who have no English, where a project worker does not speak their language;
  (b) weekend lunch club (see LASMO above);
  (c) careers workshops: CVs, presentation skills, confidence building etc.;
  (d) sporting activities: getting young people playing team sports;
  (e) visits: organizing visits to interesting places, the Houses of Parliament and museums etc.;
  (f) help for Central Office: design and print, fundraising, marketing.
- The Bankers Trust Routes Into Work Scheme is a fund which helps young people escape the benefits trap, by allowing them to accept jobs that whilst they have a low salary do get them on to the first rung of the ladder. The fund helps supplement their income so that they can still pay their rent once benefits stop.
- Glaxo Holdings are the primary partner of the Glaxo Refuge for Children at Risk, a project for under-age runaways which opened a year ago. In addition, they are working with Centrepoint to establish a project for care leavers in Ealing. They are a major funding partner, but just as importantly they will be helping to establish links with local employers in the area, to help young people access work experience and placements.
- An enthusiastic and committed group of volunteers from Royal Mail deliveries in central London help young people move on from Centrepoint projects to their own independent accommodation. After morning shifts, or at weekends, the team are often available to help load

a young person's personal belongings into a Royal Mail van and take them to their new home.

Successful companies are supporting community development through their employment practices, marketing strategies, purchasing policies, and as good corporate citizens.

Employers can ensure they are not red-lining job applications from areas of high unemployment; or unintentionally excluding long-term unemployed from applying for jobs that they might have available. Some local employers in Darlington, for example, resolved to advertise their job vacancies not just in local job centres but also in community centres and drop-in centres on estates with high unemployment, following a visit which they paid to these estates organized by the local MP, Alan Milburn. They can also run pre-recruitment or customized training programmes in which the company works with training organizations to upskill long-term unemployed for jobs that they know they are going to be recruiting for in due course.

Tyneside TEC, the Tyne & Wear Urban Development Corporations, and the Northern Development Company worked together to help Twinings, as they opened up a new factory in the North East, to train (pre-recruitment) 100 long-term unemployed.

As a marketer, companies can use their own communication channels to promote opportunities for the unemployed. Capital Radio, for example, runs a Jobs Hotline. Construction company John Laing plc, won the contract to regenerate the Holly Street estate in Hackney after being asked by the local council to tender on the basis of how they would help that council to improve the quality of life on the estate.

As a purchaser/customer of goods and services, there are opportunities to see 'if we are making rationalizations can we provide guaranteed contracts or training to help staff being made redundant, to provide us with services? Can we help community groups on council estates with high unemployment to set up enterprises to supply us?' Too idealistic? Talk to Anita Roddick about the Body Shop experience of establishing Soapworks on the Glasgow peripheral housing estate of Easterhouse.

And for construction companies, etc., doing work in areas of high unemployment, is there a local labour content?

As a good corporate citizen, companies can support projects designed to give the long-term unemployed new confidence and hope, as IBM and other companies have quietly been counselling the 'lifers' in Northern Ireland, several hundred of whom, having renounced terrorism, are gradually to be released under licence, often having spent most of their adult lives behind bars for terrorist offences. Or, for example, supporting the work of the growing number of Community Development Trusts and settlements, many of which are providing a whole range of services to their communities, from AIDS awareness counselling to hostels for the homeless.

You will notice that this is not business replacing government or local authorities. Business is not like some US 6th Cavalry in a John Wayne movie, riding over the hill, saying to government and local councils and voluntary organizations: 'Move over and we will solve these problems!' Rather, it is saying that 'We, business, may have some expertise and other resources to bring to bear on these issues alongside other partners.'

Nor is it about business running things; nor particularly about business providing cash – although sometimes that does help. And when businesses do support community activities, it is best to regard such corporate cash as social venture capital rather than replacing the Treasury.

New institutions

The Industrial Revolution produced, after a time-lag, a whole range of new social institutions to cope with the changed environment. If it is true that we are now living through the Information Revolution, whose impact will be even greater and more pervasive than the earlier Industrial Revolution, it is not unreasonable to expect that after a similar time-lag, new social institutions will emerge to meet the new environment. It is possible, however, to speed up this process and, thereby, to reduce the time-lag and to reduce the costs of transition.

The institutions that followed the Industrial Revolution reflected the values of that revolution. The characteristics of the Information Revolution are about flexibility, responding fast to change, flat organizations and virtual organizations. How do we design institutions for the future and not for the past?

Anita Halliday's chapter, the DEMOS book, *The Common Sense of Community* and the extract from the Borrie Social Justice Commission highlight, I believe correctly, the future role for Community Development Trusts. The Borrie Report also proposes a national community regeneration agency to back up and develop the work of such CDTs.

There is a danger of creating a national institution disconnected from the local manifestations. I sat as a board member of the now disbanded Co-operative Development Agency at the end of the 1980s. In retrospect, it is clear that this had little connection or engagement with local groups promoting co-operative enterprises; or mechanisms to get feedback from experts/practitioners 'at the coal-face'. It also faced problems of critical mass: because it lacked adequate resources, there were insufficient reasons for local groups to come to it. What are the lessons for how you facilitate and promote a network?

Various organizations are now helping to build capacity in community development. These include CDF, Civic Trust and the British Association of Settlements and Social Action Centres, and the National Association of Development Trusts. Business in the Community (BITC) also has activities to support community entrepreneurs (such as the community entrepreneurs development programme and Professional Firms Groups). There is still, however, a feeling of isolation between many practitioners; a lack of information or knowledge of good and/or bad practice; and an interest in ratcheting up the impact of the field.

Recent advances in information and communications technologies offer the opportunity to overcome some of these problems. The following proposals draw on BITC's current work with a group of leading information and communications technology companies on behalf of the Business Link network (one-stop shops for small business support). In this case, instead of developing the capacity of Personal Business Advisers, Information Officers and other business counsellors in the Business Links, the objective is to enhance the effectiveness of community entrepreneurs and others working in community economic development organizations.

Concept

To use information and communications technologies to:

- pull together several existing and planned information and support services for community economic development;
- commission the identification of good practice (where the information is not already available); and
- put a personal computer on the desk of every community entrepreneur in Britain (and in every Community Development Trust and settlement), together with the necessary training;
- maximize the utilization of the range of information, brokerage and training facilities accessible through the proposed programme.

From their personal computer, participants would be able to access the following:

- *Volbase:* the IBM database highlighting volunteers and volunteering opportunities.
- *Expertise database:* analogous to the IBM Volbase and based on the Professional Firms Groups of Business in the Community, Lawyers in the Community, and similar schemes organized by Action: Employees in the Community, ABSA etc.

There are analogies here to Supernet and Nearnet for Business Link: Supernet is a national scheme with an initial fifty centres of academic and technical expertise which can be tapped by the Innovation and Technology Counsellors of all the Business Links. Nearnet is the individual Business Link equivalent of Supernet which is developed by each Business Link. Longer term, the potential is for each individual

Business Link to develop particular sectoral expertise which can be tapped into by the other Business Links. A similar opportunity exists for participating community entrepreneurs and CDTs to have their own 'nearnet' which could be added to the 'Community Supernet'.

- *Provision database:* this will highlight product, equipment, premises, etc. which participating companies are prepared to make available to not-for-profit organizations. It is due to be launched by the Prince's Trust in 1995 and will broker between companies and NGOs.
- *Good practice databases:* the central organization to maintain this project would negotiate central purchasing with existing databases such as the Planning Exchange and would also be a commissioning publisher to plug information gaps. *Inter alia*, this could tap the expertise of Common Purpose, CDF, Civic Trust etc. For example, this might involve responding to queries like: Where are the ten best examples of anti-youth crime partnerships? or Where are the innovative examples of good parenting schemes? or Which CDTs have AIDS education programmes?
- *Managed bulletin board:* electronic mail facility between participating organizations for sharing of problems and of expertise. The same bulletin boards could also be used by companies and other organizations to advertise expertise, facilities etc. which they are prepared to make available to not-for-profit organizations. Companies, for example, could advertise the availability of staff doing 100-hour Management Development Assignments; or respond to third-sector agencies seeking treasurers or board members etc.
- *Community development television:* commercial organizations like BMW have their own television channel broadcasting programmes to their dealers on a regular basis (in the case of BMW, three times a week). Typical costs are £2000 per location for the hardware to receive the programmes. If the programmes are being made on a regular basis, the costs per programme are £10-15,000 per half hour and £1200 per hour to broadcast. The Media Trust is already broadcasting Voluntary Sector Television using BBC Select in the early hours of the morning. They would be an obvious partner with which to produce dedicated programming for community economic development. This might be a combination of programme segments sponsored by companies, foundations and government departments; training seminars; and briefing sessions with companies, etc.

A leading expert in Community Economic Development (CED), like the American Richard Steckel, might be filmed when lecturing at a particular CDT. This could then be broadcast and recorded by recipients for repeat use in future training programmes, etc.

There would be the facility for particular networks like British Association of Settlements and Social Action Centres (BASSAC) to make programmes just for their own networks.

The point about this is that all of the technology described here is already there, and many of the elements are already in place at least on a pilot basis.

Management

A small, central organization would be required to manage this facility, negotiate bulk purchase agreements with commercial and other sources of information for community entrepreneurs; and to provide editorial control for community enterprise television.

Funding

Initial funding is required in the form of either cash or one or more full- or part-time secondees to work up this proposal into a full project proposal.

The Prime Minister has called for some collective, national brainstorming about how to utilize the proceeds of the National Lottery. This could be an ideal candidate! Broad-scale funding could come from a combination of government, National Lottery proceeds and private sector sponsorship.

Figure 9, below, shows an analogous system established by Mercury for General Practitioners; and Figures 10a and b (pp. 113, 114) show an

Figure 9: *System for General Practitioners*

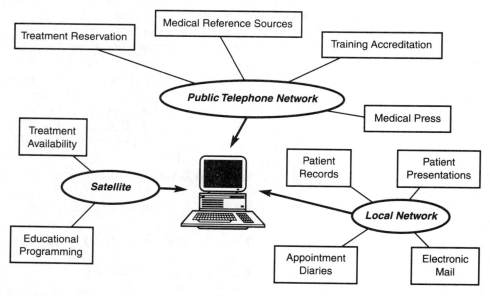

Source: *Mercury*

Figure 10a: *'Business in the Community and Business Link'*

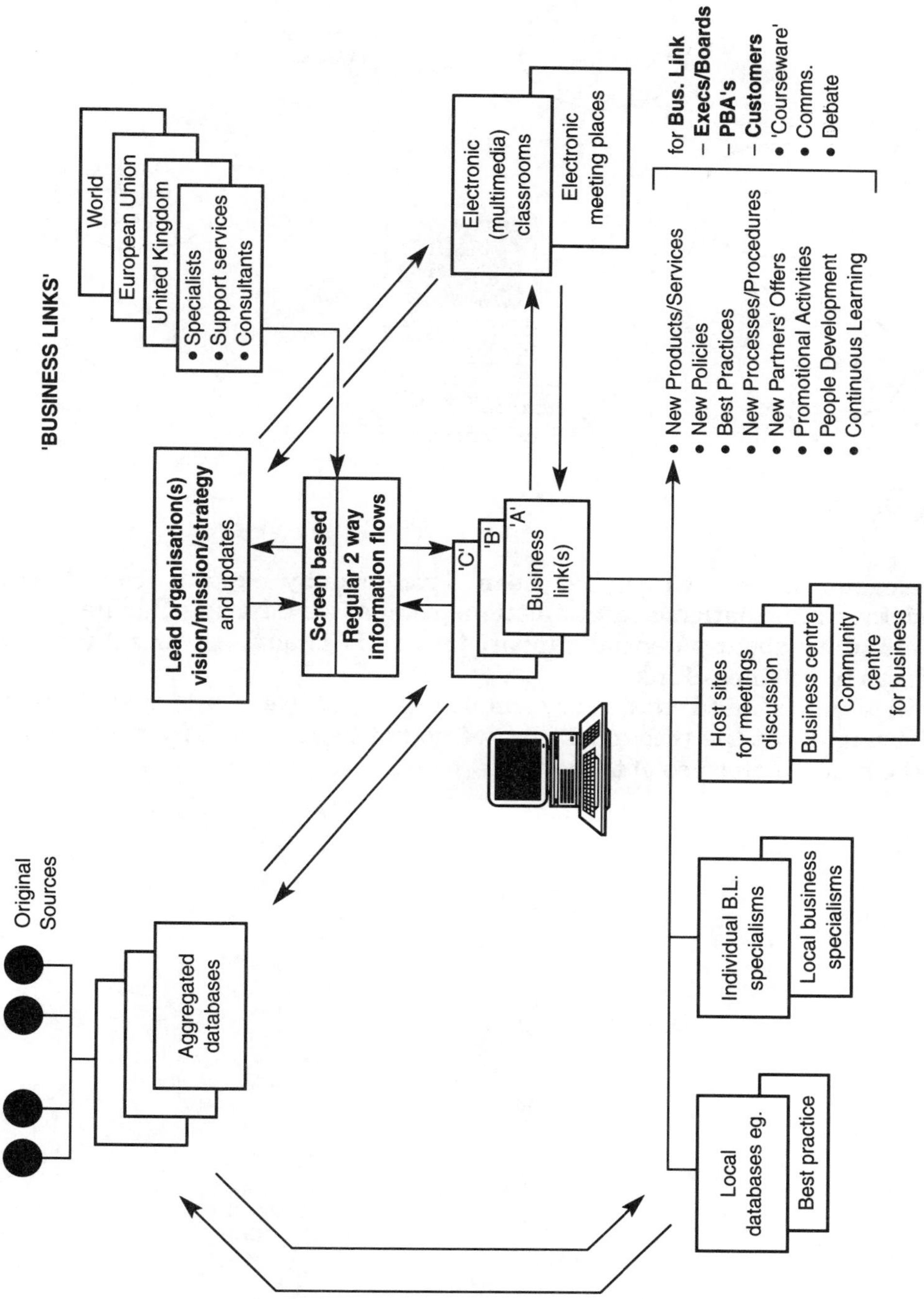

Source: *The Rio Conference, Local Agenda 21*

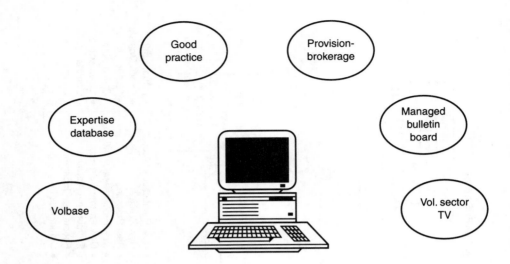

Figure 10b

analogous scheme which has been developed by experts from Mercury andother information/communications companies advising Business in the Community about potential support for business advisers and information officers in Business Link.

All of this is based on the very simple argument: we should spend less time worrying about the resources that we do not have; and more about how we make much better use of those that we do have.

18

THE SUSTAINABLE CITY

David Gee

What is the environment?

Albert Einstein said 'The environment is everything else except me.' That's rather a lot, and includes everything we get both from nature, like food, and from other people in our communities, such as work and friendship. Environmentalism is all about getting the balance right between our needs and the capacities of both nature and people to meet them, without preventing other people, elsewhere or in the future, from meeting their own needs, and without compromising the integrity of the eco-systems on which we depend. Before looking at the particular problems and opportunities of cities, let's see how dependent we are on our environment, beginning with nature.

From the first second of life, when cells come together to make a baby, we are totally dependent on our external environment – the mother's body – for our survival. After nine months on this life support system we emerge from the womb to become totally dependent on the wider and more complex environment of the earth. Just as the baby's needs in the womb can only be met within the limits of the mother's life support systems, so the needs of our species, *homo sapiens*, (the so-called 'wise ones') can only be met within the limits of the earth's capacities to sustain life.

Figure 11 (page 116) describes nature's 'life support' systems – the main products and services that we get from the web of these interconnected parts of nature – the climate, soil, vegetation, species and rocks – all working together to support and reproduce life on earth. It is clear that the *services* from nature, such as climate regulation, nutrient recycling, radiation protection (from the ozone layer in the atmosphere), are as necessary for our survival as the *products* of nature, such as food, fish and timber; but they are much harder to replace.

Shortages of nature's products such as metals and fossil fuels can be overcome by improved technology, with fewer materials being used in goods and services, or with alternative products, such as plastics from oil or olants, being used instead. The deposits of metals and fossil fuels are usually owned by someone. So, control over the preservation and supply of these products is fairly easy. Such products are also traded, and therefore have prices, which can increase, creating pressure for increased efficiency of use.

However, it is much more difficult for *homo sapiens* to deal with the loss of nature's services. It is not so easy to replace the ozone layer, or climate

Figure 11: *The main environmental products and services we get from nature*

Nature	Product service
Sun	Provides energy (warmth, light, power)
	Circulates air and water
Soil	Provides food, vegetation
	Recycles nutrients
Trees/Vegetation	Provide timber, food, medicines
	Recycle oxygen/carbon dioxide
	Bind soil, hold water
	Filter pollution
Atmosphere	Provides and circulates oxygen and nutrients
	Regulates temperature
	Blocks radiation
Animals, Insects	Provide food and clothing
	Recycle nutrients
Rocks	Provide deposits of fossil fuels, metals
	Provide soil
Oceans, Rivers, Wetlands	Provide fish and water
	Hold and circulate water
	Produce oxygen
	Store carbon dioxide
	Regulate climate
	Filter pollution
'The Countryside'	All of the above
	Recreation, peace and pleasure

regulation, or the water cycle, with clever technology. And dumping waste and pollution into the air, seas and soils can cause irretrievable damage to both nature and people, (e.g. tree death, or cancer), once a critical 'dose' of pollution is reached. Furthermore, nature's services are not owned by anybody, nor do they have prices, so that preserving them is much more difficult than dealing with shortages of products.

It is therefore the damage to nature's life support services that has led scientists and business leaders (Figure 12, page 117) to join environmentalists in concluding that we are already living beyond our ecological means.

Figure 13 (page 118) shows why these scientists and business leaders are worried. It summarizes the major ecological damage that we have managed to achieve over the last two centuries. It is clear that we are already living beyond nature's limits, particularly for ozone layer protection, fish stocks, climate regulation, water resources, acid rain, soil erosion, forest losses and for noise, air, river and land pollution. This damage varies regionally but has been caused mainly by the 1 billion people living in the rich OECD countries – less than a quarter of the current world population of 5.5 billion. As the world population grows to 8–10 billion people, with most wanting to share our living standards, then we are clearly going to greatly exceed the carrying capacity of the planet – unless we 'change course'. At the national level the

Figure 12

We are living beyond our means, say scientists ...
The Future of our planet is in the balance ... The present pattern of human activity, accentuated by population growth, should make even the most optimistic about future scientific progress pause and reconsider the wisdom of ignoring these threats to our planet. Unrestrained resource consumption for energy production and other uses, especially if the developing world strives to achieve living standards based on the same level of consumption as the developed world, could lead to catastrophic outcomes for the global environment. (*Population Growth, Resource Consumption and a Sustainable World*, Royal Society/US National Academy of Sciences, 1992)

and business leaders ...
The bottom line is that the human species is living more off the planet's capital and less off the interest. This is bad business ... many of our attempts to make progress are simply unsustainable. We cannot continue in our present methods of using energy, managing forests, farming, protecting plant and animal species, managing urban growth and producing industrial goods. Sustainable development is ... about redefining the rules of the economic game in order to move from a situation of wasteful consumption and pollution to one of conservation, and from one of privilege and protectionism to one of fair and equitable chances to all. No one can reasonably doubt that fundamental change is needed. (*Changing Course: a Global Business Perspective on Development and the Environment*, Business Council on Sustainable Development, MIT, 1992)

---

state of our environment gives little cause for complacency, with air and water pollution, species loss, habitat destruction, acid rain and other eco-problems remaining unsolved or getting worse, despite the other improvements that are being made, such as bathing water quality, and land under conservation (New Economics Foundation, FOE, etc. 1994).

If our eco-systems are over-stressed, what about the people part of our environment, our social systems? We don't have to look far to see that many of our social support systems are also breaking down, and that unemployment, crime, divorce, child abuse, immorality, homelessness, social exclusion, discrimination, poverty and ill health are some of the most damaging results. Ethnic minorities, women and, increasingly, children, feel excluded, or at least marginalized, and society becomes fragmented. The 'common good' is difficult to see. If 'everything except me' is breaking up it is not surprising that many people are cracking up themselves, or at least feeling powerless to change things for the better. And this is especially so in cities where the concentration of people and their activities puts particular stress on both the natural and social support systems.

Cities – the focus for action

About 80% of Europeans live or work in urban areas and many of them experience the pollution, congestion, unemployment, poverty, homelessness, social exclusion and crime that are a feature of urban life. The decline of manufacturing and ports has led to the spiritual and economic decline of

Figure 13: *Two centuries of ecological damage – world and Europe.*

	World	Europe
Soil/land degradation	15–20%	20–25%
Habitat loss	20–25%	70–80%
Forests destroyed	20–30%	90%
Amount of remaining forest degraded/damaged	5–10%	50–70%
Ozone layer (seasonal losses)	4–5%	10–14%
Salt marshes – area lost	50%	–
Coral reefs – polluted/destroyed	5–10%	–
Animal/bird species threatened	10–12%	10–15%
Acid rain – area affected	–	75%
Acid rain – amount above critical load	–	20 times
Global warming gases – reduction needed	60%	90%
Major fishing areas – over-fished	100%	100%
Freshwater fish species – extinct/endangered	20%	40%
Pollution – of groundwater	–	100%
Pollution – air in major cities	25%	100%

Source: *World Resources 1994–5 – a Guide to the Global Environment.* World Resources Institute; *State of the World 1993 & 1994*, Worldwatch Institute, USA.

many European cities, accompanied by the dereliction of land and buildings, and a deterioration in the social and natural environment. Even where cities are prospering, the quality of life is declining due to air pollution, noise congestion, stress and communities being fractured by roads and large developments. What is harder to see is the 'eco-impact' that the city has on more distant parts, as the city sucks in resources from around the world, and dumps its wastes as far away as possible. The 'ecological footprint' of cities and urban areas is huge – studies from the Netherlands and Canada (Rees and Wackernagel, 1994) show that cities consume the resources and waste capacities of land areas that are ten to twenty times the area they occupy.

But if cities are at the centre of unsustainable eco-nomic behaviour they also provide opportunities for harnessing the energies and imagination of thousands of people who want to act locally to improve their environments. All across Europe people in communities are beginning to create different ways of living and working that rebuild the fabric of their natural and social environments. They are trying to put meaning, purpose, quality and morals back into their lives. They may not talk about the environmentalists' goal of 'sustainable development', which is 'about delivering basic environmental, social and economic services to residents of a community, without threatening the viability of the natural, built and social systems upon which the delivery of these services depends' (International Council for Local Environmental Initiatives – ICLEI), but they are heading that way.

Many of these initiatives are completely 'bottom up', such as the anti-roads campaigns arising particularly from the Twyford Down battle in 1992. This has now developed nationwide and is being co-ordinated by ALARM UK and the Road Alert campaigns. Elsewhere there are experiments in 'Local exchange trading schemes' (LETS) that use locally invented currencies to account for the swapping of skills and work between those who have neither conventionally paid work nor much money. There are now over three hundred LETS schemes in the UK, as well as dozens of other experiments in local currency circulation such as community banks and credit unions. In the USA people have also started another kind of currency scheme called Time Dollars which are earned by providing care for others in the local area but which can only be 'spent' on care for oneself or one's friends or relatives.

There are also over 1400 community enterprises in cities and other areas which, over the last two decades, have asked the question 'What can we do?' and have decided 'to take action on their own account rather than wait for someone else to come and do it for them'. Many of these are not 'green' in the traditional sense but they are to do with the natural, built or social environment that Einstein defined, meeting local needs for employment and services that the conventional economy was failing to provide.

Others are trying to support local farmers by buying their food directly from them, delivered through community organized 'box' schemes, or paid for via consumer subscription schemes; and at the other end of our food chain, promoting home composting schemes. Others are building their houses with the help of groups like the Walter Segal Trust; reclaiming open spaces, or cleaning polluted streams with the help of Groundwork Trusts; or improving home insulation with assistance from Neighbourhood Energy Action.

Many other initiatives involve partnerships between communities and their local authorities, often organized around 'Local Agenda 21' campaigns. These have developed out of the recommendations of the Rio Conference on Environment and Development in 1992 (Figure 14, below), which laid down a world programme for achieving sustainable development in the next century. Many towns and cities have responded enthusiastically to the local component of this new agenda.

The Local Government Management Board is co-ordinating Local Agenda 21 activities in the UK. Most of the 540 local authorities have appointed Environmenal Co-ordinators (175 to date), and many have started the consultation with their communities over implementing Agenda 21 locally. European action is being co-ordinated by the ICLEI and by the European Sustainable Cities and Towns campaign that grew out of the Aarlberg Conference and Charter on Sustainable Cities in 1993. In the UK the 'Recycling Cities' of the Friends of the Earth/British Telecom initiative, Sheffield, Cardiff, and Dundee, have been joined by the Royal Society for Nature Conservation/BT, 'Sustainable Cities' of Leeds, Leicester, Middlesbrough and Peterborough, and by others who are creating their own Local Agenda 21 programmes, such as Coventry, Blackburn, Brighton, Southampton, Sutton and many others on the continent.

Figure 14

AGENDA 21
Chapter 28
'Local authorities' initiatives in support of Agenda 21'

28.1 Because so many of the problems and solutions being addressed by Agenda 21 have their roots in local activities, the participation and co-operation of local authorities will be a determining factor in fulfilling its objectives.

As the level of governance closest to the people, they play a vital role in educating, mobilizing and responding to the public to promote sustainable development.

a. By 1996, most local authorities in each country should have undertaken a consultative process with their populations and achieved a consensus on a 'local Agenda 21' for the community . . .

d. All local authorities in each country should be encouraged to implement and monitor programmes which aim at ensuring that women and youth are represented in decision-making, planning and implementation processes.

Activities
28.3. Each local authority should enter into a dialogue with its citizens, local organizations, and private enterprises and adopt a 'local Agenda 21'. Through consultation and consensus-building, local authorities would learn from citizens and from local, civic, community, business and industrial organizations and acquire the information needed for formulating the best strategies.

The International Council for Local Environmental Initiatives (ICLEI) which helped draft Chapter 28 of Agenda 21, has produced guidelines for implementing Local Agenda 21 and is developing a model programme in co-operation with 21 local authorities from Southern and Northern hemispheres. Two European countries, the UK and Finland, have national co-ordinating committees for their local Agenda 21 activity.

Cities like Freiberg, Copenhagen, Aarlberg, Berlin, Bremen, Bilbao, Stockholm, Evora, the Emscher Park area of the Ruhr, and Orebro are pioneering new ways of reducing dependency on the car, creating employment within small and medium-sized firms, reducing waste, providing green spaces, renovating derelict areas, stimulating the local production and distribution of food, developing renewable energy production and energy efficiency schemes, and building eco-efficient homes.

The employment consequences of many of these initiatives can be considerable. For example, the Danish projects to improve energy efficiency in homes, to recycle electronic and demolition waste, as well as to recycle rainwater, develop renewable energies and generally to carry out eco-renovation on homes and neighbourhoods, is generating the UK equivalent of one million jobs. In each case the usually separated worlds of health, employment, energy, transport, housing and environment are coming together. And all of these initiatives involve the 'bottom up' mobilization of people in their different communities. As Aarlberg City Council concluded, 'Environmental problems are essentially social and cultural problems. Technical solutions alone will not work. The aware and involved citizen will be able to reach the heart of the problem, which is the individual's excessive consumption of resources and the inadequate management of waste materials.'

Barriers to sustainability

Much can be achieved by individual efforts but there are also limits to local initiatives that come from the overall political, administrative, cultural and economic systems, which encourage unsustainable activity. Reducing car use, for example, is only feasible if there are alternative means of transport and a reduced need to travel long distances between home, work, leisure and services. Three features of our socio-economic systems stand out particularly as barriers to successful community action on the environment.

The first is the conventional value system which is characterized by individualism, short-termism, departmentalism and materialism, all of which militate against hitting the right balance between our needs and the environment's capacity to meet them. The second is the way of perceiving the world. As Aristotle said, 'before action comes perception' and the kind of action we take is influenced by the way we see the world. Conventional ways of seeing, such as perceiving problems of transport, health, housing, environment and employment as separate problems, with their associated specialisms, departmental budgets and cultures, prevent us seeing the inter-connections in the whole system.

The third is an economic system that is largely divorced from the real world of resources and people, has prices that do not reflect the full costs of production and consumption, and a tax system that encourages the waste of both people and nature.

Preconditions for sustainability

The seeds of the future are being sown by the local initiatives described above which are taking root despite the soil of unsustainability in which they find themselves. As with nature, new growth develops amongst the decay of the old. However, the new growth can be nurtured and accelerated by removing the two barriers to sustainability, namely conventional values and perceptions.

Values

Figure 15 (page 122) describes the environmental values needed for sustainability, and contrasts them with conventional values. Both sets of values are important – it's just the balance between them that needs to shift towards environmental values if we are to stem environmental decline and make a better world for us all.

Figure 15: *The role of values and perceptions in environmental management.*

Value/perceptions about:	Conventional	Environmental
Nature	Collection of separate physical things	An inter-connected living system
	Dependent on the Economy	Economy dependent on Nature
	Infinite	Finite
People and Power	Individualistic	Part of Communities
	Competitive	Cooperative
	Independent	Inter-dependent
	Consumer	Citizen
	Have Material only	Have Non-Material Needs, Too
	Homo Sapiens	*Homo Stupidus*
	Centralised	Decentralised
Relation of Nature to People	People-Centred	Species-centred
	Subdue and Conquer	Nurture and Conserve
	Exploit and Forget	Use and Respect
	Knowable	Unknowable
Industry	Maximise Profits for Shareholders	Optimise Returns to Stakeholders
	Short-Termist	Long-Termist
	Dump, or Clean Up, Pollution	Minimise Waste
	Maximise Productivity of labour	Maximize Productivity of Nature
	"S and F" = Sell and Forget	"L and R" = Lease and Return, Restore, Recycle, Renovate
	Sell Products	Sell Services

Perceptions

There are ten new ways of seeing the world that will help put us on the road to sustainability.

1. *The environment is everything except me.* The environment is not just about green spaces and nature but about equity (both between groups now, and future generations); the relations between people; and their social, cultural and built environments.
2. *Everything connects.* Reality is inter-connected, so policies, budgets and political structures have to be integrated as they are in people's lives. As one poor pensioner said after months of battling over his fuel poverty, 'the only place where health, housing and energy come together is in my life'. And this also means that partnerships between industry, community groups, local and national government, and the EU are essential.
3. *Think circular, not linear.* Nature works in circles with wastes becoming food, and with closed cycles of water, carbon, nitrogen, etc. helping the world go round. *Homo stupidus*, at least since the Industrial Revolution, has been thinking and behaving in straight lines: make a product (and

lots of waste), sell it, forget it, dump it and start again. Cities suck resources and energy in then spew out wastes. Many companies are now thinking and planning to sell *services* (use of solvents, cars rather than products), and to recycle, re-use and renovate products. One company's wastes can be another's resources, which again means partnerships and communication where there was once isolation. Cities are planning much greater use of combined heat and power, and of renewable energy. They are organizing the recycling of demolition waste, rainwater, electronic waste, as well as of glass, metals and paper. Community banking, currency and credit systems are based around the local circulation of money, rather than on the once-through system of money passing straight to the international financial markets.

4. *Matter matters as much as money.* Energy, water, food, materials and money flow through cities, companies and countries but it is only money that gets measured and monitored, giving us only a partial understanding of the real economy. This is as bad as trying to understand the biology of an animal by only monitoring its blood circulation and ignoring the throughput of food, its digestion and disposal. By failing to properly account for the use of energy and natural capital, such as the depreciation of oil, trees and soil, we give ourselves a misleadingly high impression of wealth and 'progress'. We therefore need resource accounts (with resource productivity ratios, etc.) at city, company and national level, alongside financial accounts, so that we get a more complete understanding and, therefore, control of the real economy.

5. *Let's put the 'eco' back into eco-nomic.* The economy is totally dependent on the environment. There can be no economy without an environment but there can be environments without economies. Over the last hundred years or so conventional economics has lost its roots in the resource base of the material world, which helps to explain why we have gone beyond the carrying capacity of the earth in key areas like ozone protection, soil integrity and tree growth. A load on a ship can be arranged 'efficiently' but if it is too much for the carrying capacity of the ship it still sinks – efficiently. We need 'ecological Plimsoll lines' for the eco-nomy that would keep the throughput of energy and materials below the damage thresholds for the environment. These may be more difficult to work out than ship loading lines but its a more pleasant job than trying to save ourselves once the ship has capsized.

6. *Let's pay for the present.* The prices of energy, food, transport and other goods do not reflect all the costs of their production and consumption. The full costs of transport, for example, include congestion, accidents, noise, pollution, respiratory disease, etc., but these huge costs, estimated to be around 4% of GNP for the EU countries, are not captured in the price of cars or fuel. This means that there is no market incentive to reduce these costs. Economists call environmental damage

costs 'externalities' because they are external to the financial accounts of the company or customer. Pollution costs are real costs being borne by real people, either victims, taxpayers, future generations, or all three, but they are not part of the normal market economy. This distorts investment decisions in favour of the 'cheap' products such as car transport, energy and mass-produced food. Most politicians and business leaders now recognize the need to 'internalize externalities' if the economy is not to be a barrier to sustainability.

7. *Tax 'bads' not 'goods'.* About two-thirds of the government's tax revenue comes from the activities of people at work in businesses, and savers/investors, and only one-third comes from the consumption of resources. Yet over the last two decades the taxes on people (economic 'goods') have risen a lot whilst the taxes on resources and pollution (environmental 'bads') have declined. As a result, the economy over-consumes the cheap resource, nature, and under-consumes the expensive resource, people, leaving us with both eco-damage and unemployment. This is not what we want. As the EU White Paper on Growth, Competitiveness and Employment observed, the inadequate use of resources – too little labour, too much use of environmental resources – is clearly 'not in line with the preferences of society . . . people expect for themselves and their children not only more jobs and a stable income but also a higher quality of life'. We need a new structure of taxes and prices that would help us to employ rather more of people and rather less of nature. Eco-nomic Tax Reform (ETR) entails shifting, over a ten- or fifteen-year period, a large proportion of taxes from the activities of people (by the abolition of national insurance tax, and the lowering of income and profits taxes, etc.) and on to the use and misuse of resources (by taxes on energy, transport, pollution, and wastes), so that the economy is re-focused on to employment and 'eco-efficiency'. (WBMG, 1994)

8. *Manage, not meet, demand.* We used to meet the demand for energy solely by increasing the supply from power stations, until we realized that the need for heat, light and warmth could also be met by energy efficiency and conservation, and this could often be cheaper than new energy supply. 'Negawatts', or demand side management, not megawatts, or supply provision, became the goal of energy investment, particularly in America. Similarly, the demand for cars used to be met almost exclusively by increasing the supply of roads, but congestion and the other costs of cars are now persuading planners to think of reducing the demand for mobility by improving access to jobs, homes, shops, leisure and public transport so that we have less dependence on the car. There are policy and price barriers to managing not meeting demand, but most of these are dealt with above.

9. *Development need not mean more (quantity), just better (quality).* Once people reach about 18 years of age they stop growing. They then don't

stagnate but continue to develop for the rest of their lives. Mature economies, like people, could stop worrying about continuous expansion in size, and focus on providing the basics of jobs, homes, a supportive environment, and non-material needs. A continuous swelling in the size of the economy does not necessarily mean we are better off. The economy has grown a lot over the last fifteen years but life has got worse for many people. All the studies of what makes people content with life show that there is no relation between happiness and growth in the economy. We should concentrate on what people want – work, shelter, food, and fun – rather than on growing faster in the hope that their needs will be met from 'growth'. More does not always mean better.

One of the founding fathers of eco-nomics, John Stuart Mill wrote: 'I am inclined to believe that it (the stationary state of capital and wealth) would on the whole be a very considerable improvement on our present condition. . . . It is scarcely necessary to remark that a stationary state of capital and population implies no stationary state of human improvement. There would be as much scope as ever for all kinds of mental culture, and moral and social progress; as much room for improving the Art of Living, and much more likelihood of its being improved' (*Principles of Political Economy*, 1857).

10. *Measure and monitor real progress.* The GNP is the god of progress, yet it is false. It ignores the depreciation of natural capital, such as oil, soils and trees; it counts more pollution and clean up as more progress: it ignores the distribution of the benefits of growth, so that the increased inequalities of the last decade are not counted; and it ignores all work that does not have a wage, such as bringing up the next generation, or looking after the sick or elderly at home. And it ignores the quality of life. As President Kennedy noted: 'The gross national product does not allow for the health of our children, the quality of their education, or the joy of their play . . . It measures neither wit nor our courage; neither our wisdom or our learning; neither our compassion or our devotion to our country; it measures everything in short, except that which makes life worthwhile' (Robert F. Kennedy, *Recapturing America's Moral Vision*, 18 March 1968).

We need new ways of measuring both national progress, like the 'Index of Sustainable Economic Welfare' (Figure 15, page 122, which corrects the GNP for most of its deficiencies, and which shows that overall welfare has declined since the mid-1970s (Jackson and Marks, 1994)), and new ways of judging local progress, like the Seattle 'Sustainable Community Indicators' now being adapted by several local communities in the UK (UNA, 1994). These are 'bottom up' measures which people design themselves to reflect what they think is important, such as fish returning to the local rivers, jobs, clean air and being able to see surrounding hills again.

Figure 16: *Index of Sustainable Economic Welfare for the United Kingdom, 1950-1990*

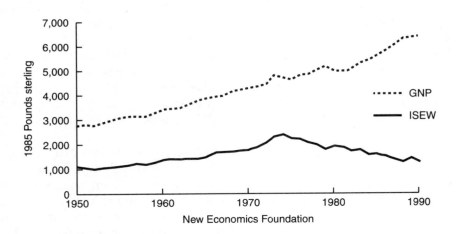

New Economics Foundation

Source: *New Economics Foundation*

Conclusion

The global market is failing people and their environments in most parts of the world. People are beginning to respond to their unmet needs by constructing new ways of working and living that go some way to regenerating local communities. Both the global and local environmental problems can be addressed by community action for sustainable cities and settlements, but only if new values, new perceptions and new eco-nomics allow free rein to the innovations and energies that community movements are generating. These movements are tiny; the ideas are not new, but in the context of the failure of national political parties to deliver, they are likely to grow. They offer the hope of an alternative to the gathering forces of reaction which are tempting increasingly desperate people with the simple, but dangerous slogans of nationalism, exclusion and 'strong government'.

COMMUNITY – THE GOVERNMENT AND POLITICAL BUILDING BLOCKS

*If community is to be strengthened and
neighbourhoods are to become more self-reliant,
then government must become enabling.
To do that it needs to evolve new structures and fresh attitudes.*

19

ENABLING STRUCTURES

Henry Tam

Citizens and government institutions

Citizens have for too long been regarded as mere subjects of the state. Having supposedly given our tacit consent to an endless range of activities which affect our lives being run by a centralized government, we were meant to be content so long as it was possible for us to elect different people to be in charge of that government. In practice, quite apart from the difficulties one has in trying to make any difference with one's vote outside a marginal seat, the fact remains that when one group of politicians manages to displace another, the monopolistic power to govern simply passes from one to the other.

The increasing disillusionment with narrow party politics and the remote state apparatus ensconced in Whitehall has in recent years led many people across the political spectrum to demand a new approach to government. In line with this demand, citizens would no longer be treated as passive recipients of state services; instead, everyone is to be encouraged to play an active role in shaping those diverse activities which constitute governance in this country.

In this chapter, we will look at what may be termed the empowering approach to government, an approach which can be characterized by three key features:

1. Giving citizens the power to influence governmental activities which affect their lives.
2. Giving citizens more power to deal with their own individual and community concerns.
3. Giving citizens the power to protect their interests in relation to organizations not under the direct control of the state sector.

We will focus on local government both because it is the level of government most accessible to the public and because it is uniquely placed to provide civic leadership in rebuilding communities, without which citizenship cannot fully develop.

In the last ten years, local government has been at the forefront of a series of major political and managerial changes. These changes have led many to take a new look at how those who provide public services and those who directly or indirectly benefit from such services should relate to each other. This does not mean that local government is now doing all the right things; on the contrary, the experience to date shows that whilst the consensus on good practice is growing amongst the most forward-thinking authorities, there is still not enough commitment to drive the message home to others which have not yet shaken off their old hierarchical attitudes. In pointing out how the empowering approach can be developed, this chapter may add to the momentum to transform the relationship between citizens and government institutions, both locally and nationally.

Developing an empowering corporate culture

The place to start building such an empowering approach is within the corporate culture of each local authority. Unless elected members and senior officers can demonstrate their commitment to empowerment within the organization, they are not likely to persuade many staff to engage wholeheartedly in such an approach in relation to the public. It is important to remember that people who work for local authorities are also citizens of the locality. If those who have the power in the prevailing structure refuse to involve others in their organizations in the exercise of that power, then citizens outside the formal structure of those organizations are even less likely to attain any meaningful involvement.

There are five aspects of cultural development which are essential. First, the concept of empowering citizens must be built into the core values of the local authority. The statement of such values ought to be simple but clear for all staff to see. The central message, however expressed, is that the authority respects and welcomes the views of others in determining its activities. It has no monopoly of wisdom and therefore it embraces partnership with citizens who work in the authority, with citizens as service users, and with citizens collectively in the form of community groups.

Secondly, everyone brought into the authority must, through the initial induction process and ongoing training support thereafter, learn about the meaning and practical implications of empowerment. Many local authorities have taken on board the importance of customer care training. But they will need to move on from looking after the needs of their customers as they perceive them, to working with their customers in determining what those needs are and how they are best met from the perspective of the customers themselves.

Thirdly, communications between staff at all levels must be open, regular and effective. Those delivering services need to be informed of not just the policy requirements but the reasons behind those requirements; this means that they can in turn put forward suggestions on what needs to be changed, or where improvements can be made. Where communications have not been effectively opened up, a formal suggestion scheme may help to break the ice. It is easy to overlook internal communications when one is pressing for more extensive co-operation between local government and local citizens but without the former put on a sound basis, any push for the latter would soon lead to disillusionment when it becomes clear that the authority in question is not capable of responding swiftly and openly to ideas put forward by others.

The fourth aspect involves giving staff the motivation to respond to the concerns of those they serve in the most effective manner. In practice this would involve giving staff greater flexibility and autonomy in running their own service areas. Provided the overall objectives of those service areas are clearly defined through a regular and two-way performance appraisal, staff should be allowed to devise their own solutions with minimal intervention from other levels of the authority. Structurally and culturally, this is a key element of any strategy to open up the organization to citizens who do not hold any of the traditional decision-making positions.

Finally, local authority staff should be encouraged to take a wider interest in their local communities and be given the support to develop their skills to carry out not just their formal functions within the authority but also in areas which can benefit community groups, such as skills in running independent trusts, putting together bid proposals for grants and donations, or carrying out cost-effective planning and monitoring of voluntary activities.

The democratic role of public information

Building on the empowering corporate culture which has been developed with all those working within a given local authority, an infrastructure for democratic communications with those outside the council can be constructed. Isolation and alienation are often the result of communications breakdown. In many cases, there are public agencies, community groups, or caring individuals who would step in to help if only they knew about the problems. Local authorities can play a vital role in ensuring that information necessary for the public good is made available through the most effective communications network.

However, any attempt to increase the flow of public information has to tread a careful path between being excessively detailed and hence dull on the one hand, and being selectively emotive and thus resembling propaganda on the other. What is needed is a sensitive application of the communications techniques developed by marketing and public relations professionals to the domain of information sharing in a democratic community.

Local authorities and their respective citizens may find it useful to refer to the following checklist as a starting point for measuring the adequacy of public information provision in their area:

- Information on local people's rights so that they are clear about their entitlements.
- Information on their responsibilities so that they know what is required of them.
- Information which helps them manage their lives more effectively.
- Information on new developments and opportunities for them to give their views.
- Information to enhance their awareness of what is happening in their communities and the conditions of their fellow citizens.
- Information as part of an ongoing dialogue between local government and local citizens concerning key policy issues.

If the above range of information is to be readily available for all citizens, then they must be proactively provided. One of the most serious fallacies to be rejected is based on the claim that apathy justifies ignorance. According to this fallacy, giving local people free public information is a waste of public money because people are not interested in such information. But it is precisely ignorance which breeds apathy! If citizens are to have an informed input into the deliberations which affect their lives, the vicious circle of ignorance-to-apathy-to-more-ignorance must be broken up. In any case, experience up and down the country has confirmed that when a steady flow of public information has been established, local people not only appreciate the availability of the information but they become far more ready to give their response and comments on public issues.

In order to make the proactive provision of information effective, local people should be given every opportunity to have an input at the planning stage. This must not be confined to some one-off questionnaire which is likely to be binned, but developed as part of a long-term strategy to involve local people in identifying issues of real concern to them.

Community involvement can also play a particularly important role in disseminating the information which is produced after consultation with local citizens. This is an area where even the strongest commitment to act can fall down because of the lack of understanding of how information is best targeted. Four types of channel deserve greater attention from both local authorities and third-sector organizations which are playing an increasingly important role in involving ordinary citizens in the process of local self-government. The four types of public information channels which need to be developed are as follows.

Community information points

Information should be given out where local people gather. To date local authorities have concentrated on libraries because these happen to be within their direct management control but in the future more information points would have to be identified and developed regardless of who has direct management control over them.

Community newspapers

Many local authorities are now producing their own council newspapers, but they have a long way to go before these publications become genuine vehicles for local people to determine what information affecting their communities would be made readily available.

Direct mail via community database

One of the problems frequently encountered in community liaison work is that there is no regularly updated 'Who's who' directory for the local statutory and voluntary bodies. Local authorities should take the lead in establishing a computer database which will not only be regularly updated but which can be used to target direct mail information to different groups and individuals in the community.

E-mail network between local authorities and community groups

Once a comprehensive database is in place, it would be worth considering how an e-mail network can be developed. The administrative chores of sending out hundreds or even thousands of documents in hard copy for information or comments can be replaced by split-second on-screen communications. Roads and buildings are familiar items in requests for infrastructural development but information technology must also be added to the list for future community development.

From responsive to participatory government

The combination of an empowering corporate culture within the local authority and a well-informed public across the local community provides an excellent basis for responsive government. The extent to which responsive government is being achieved can be measured by the local authority's performance in relation to the following:

- Enquiries and requests for action are dealt with promptly and effectively.
- Complaints are welcome, systematically identified and resolved.

- Opportunities are available for suggestions on where improvements can be made.
- The changing needs and expectations of citizens are regularly identified and anticipated through the appropriate application of customer research techniques.

But even responsive government is only a stage towards a fully empowering approach. The ultimate goal must be the involvement of more and more people in determining matters which are of concern primarily to them. Far from undermining the authority of elected politicians or the professional judgments of officials, greater participation by informed citizens enhances local government's abilities to act in the best possible interest of local people.

Citizenship development

The more forward-thinking local authorities have in recent years been formulating citizenship development strategies as part of their overall corporate strategies. Braintree, Portsmouth, York, Middlesbrough and others have sought to increase the opportunities citizens have in influencing their local government. They also recognize that if the new opportunities are to be fully utilized, citizens must be given every encouragement to try out the experience of participation.

One of the starting-points is public involvement in council and committee meetings. However, if this is to succeed, the council concerned must focus on how to get local people to take an interest in the proceedings and not fall into the trap of equating the inevitably low initial turnout with some inexplicably inherent problem with participatory democracy.

For many residents, taking part in customer advisory groups which consider council services with which they are directly familiar may be a better introduction to how local government works. Such advisory groups are already instrumental in the development of customer contracts, review of service standards, and quality audit. In taking part, citizens learn about the issues which are central to evaluating the activities of their local government, and gain vital experience in making decisions which impact on the quality of life in their communities.

Local authorities can further support citizens who participate in these groups by giving them training to enhance their skills and knowledge in analysing policy and management issues and in conducting group deliberations to reach democratic decisions.

Power sharing

Citizenship development initiatives have a crucial role to play in paving the way for constructive power sharing between local government and the people it serves. One of the most commonly cited barriers to power sharing is that people outside government have neither the understanding nor sense of responsibility to be entrusted with any significant share of governmental power. In fact, most people respond positively when given real responsibility to deal with important issues. The experience of being entrusted with important matters affecting the whole community in turn strengthens the sense of civic responsibility.

Local authorities can enter into power sharing partnerships by a variety of means. It is worth noting that authorities which have experimented with wider power sharing with their electorate have tended to extend their experiments rather than reverse back to a monopolistic approach to govern- ance. Decentralization of managerial functions to area offices are ideal preludes to devolution of decision-making power to neighbourhood commit- tees, on which co-opted as well as elected members can serve.

One of the real difficulties in developing power sharing in any community is that in practice it is impossible for everyone to be equally active in sharing the power on offer. This means that some may have a far greater influence on the political process than others. However, instead of accepting this as a justification for retreating from power sharing, the way to tackle it is to spread the opportunities for power sharing as widely as possible and to monitor to ensure that no groups are being left out.

In addition to neighbourhood committees, partnerships can be set up with community groups either to undertake specific projects or to consider certain strategic issues (e.g. crime prevention, environmental protection, local enterprise). A plurality of partnerships and panels will help to involve as many different community interests as possible.

Power transfer

Power sharing not only improves local authorities' understanding of local people's views on major issues, it also enables local people to demonstrate their abilities to play a responsible part in the political process. Where it is not necessary to retain a formal input from the local authority, the question of power transfer could quite properly be raised.

Anyone who is remotely acquainted with the debate about the UK's position in the European Union has heard the argument that Brussels should not be allowed to take control of any matter which can be effectively dealt with at a more local level. Whitehall has been keen to deploy this argument to ensure that power is concentrated at the national rather than the European level because the former is more local than the latter. However, by the same token, many functions undertaken by central govern- ment at the moment should be transferred to local government as they can be effectively dealt with at the more local level. Furthermore, the scope of transfer should not stop there. The principle of subsidiarity should be followed through to local groups which can take over specific responsibilities hitherto held by local government departments.

In education, the delegation of budget management to schools has meant that parents and governors have a more direct influence on setting the priorities on what to finance in their own schools. In housing, tenants' groups on a number of estates have been given support to set up their own management associations to determine how they want to run their own estates. The running of community facilities has also been handed over in many areas to management committees comprising local people who either use those facilities or have a good knowledge of those who do on a regular basis. The point is taken to its logical conclusion in the next chapter.

Meanwhile, considerable work remains to be done to translate equal opportunities policies into effective codes of practice for citizens' participation in the exercise of local political power. Such codes should be developed with the active involvement of all sections of the community and they need to be backed by training and monitoring resources to ensure that they are followed in practice. The end product could be a local constitution which sets out how political power locally is to be distributed, checked, shared and where appropriate, transferred. It would mark a significant step from the service charters which are beginning to proliferate, to a community constitution for local self-government.

The way forward

Local authorities have an important part to play in providing a democratic anchor in every local community in this country. Where fragmentation, apathy and confusion may have hitherto predominated, they can take the lead in restoring community pride. By moving their corporate culture in the empowering direction, by improving their public information provision, by enhancing participatory government through power sharing and power transfer, they can give communities the strength and confidence to take charge of their own affairs.

Central government needs to respond to this in three ways. First, it must learn to trust and support the granting of power and responsibilities to local authorities wherever they concern matters which are best dealt with at the more local level. Secondly, they should take on board the lessons which pioneering local authorities have learnt from involving citizens in their policy and service development deliberations. In many respects, central government is still light years behind what the best local authorities understand by open government. Thirdly, in parallel to a better understanding of what is best left to more local institutions, central government should concentrate more on the nationwide strategic issues which need to be tackled. Even the best partnership between local authorities and their citizens would not work if central government fails to deal with the problems which exist at the national level.

The empowering approach to government can transform the hierarchical relationship between citizens and the state into a co-operative network of community partnerships from the local, through the national, to the level of the European Union and beyond. It will need the support of national politicians but most of all it will need to be driven by local authorities working in partnership with local citizens.

20

ADDING PARTICIPATION TO REPRESENTATION

Dick Atkinson

Before residents can act as serious partners with their local authority their robust enterprising neighbourhoods need to be given an outward expression. How can the many urban villages from which each town is built, be excavated from beneath the accumulated concrete jungle and exert their identity upon the physical, social and economic geography of tomorrow? The following suggestions form only a brief introductory answer which might begin to name and assert the sense of place and identity of each neighbourhood or urban village.

As the charity Common Ground has shown, urban villages need boundaries, clear entry and exit points. There is sense in making these obvious and distinctive, like postal district signs so that residents and visitors can know when they are being 'welcomed' within these boundaries or invited to return upon leaving. They also need a central focal point. It does not matter whether the centre is identified by shops, a library, a school or community centre as long as it is clear to residents where this centre is and as long as it has the right atmosphere, either because of its architecture or the quality of the services which it offers, or both. Perhaps a distinctive flag, crest or shield might help to give identity to both the entry gateways and the central features of the village.

At Christmas, Diwali, carnival time or during some other local celebration, both gateways and central features might be enhanced by festive decorations, perhaps prepared by schools, or religious organizations, residents' groups or other voluntary organizations. The content and style of the celebrations will, of course, differ according to the particular community; but whatever their content, they are important occasions and the more people that take part in the planning and execution of them the better. Such occasions can represent the strength of the community in a variety of forms including sport, art and business as well as being purely social or religious events. They can serve to highlight calendar festivals and mark the natural passing of the seasons which urban life otherwise obscures.

A building, whether it is a library, school, Trust or shopping centre, which functions as a village hall and a meeting place and the open space which represents the village green or some kind of arena are important, not only to host celebrations but to serve the needs of different interest groups. Community notice boards and community newspapers can advertise events and spread local news and information, providing the village with its own voice while also helping to promote local businesses and schools. A supplement to the newspaper might form a 'welcome package' for those moving into the area and introduce them to the local amenities and their neighbours.

Buildings and developments which affect the life of the village often do not take enough account of its particular identity or of the wishes of residents. It would be profitable to build and develop in ways which highlight that identity rather than inhibit, depress or destroy it. The style and proportions of buildings, the materials used and the location of facilities are all crucial to the creation of harmony in a neighbourhood as well as a sense of history, continuity and belonging.

Nothing is ever perfect or complete. Perhaps with the help of a Planning for Real exercise, different villages might come to assert one or other mix of the attributes outlined above, but few will have the possibility of being purpose designed and built as is the case with Poundbury, a village which is being constructed on farmland on the edge of the small town of Dorchester. The idea was conceived by Prince Charles with the help of the architect Leon Krier; they hope that the new village will eventually comprise some two thousand homes housing a population of eight thousand. A key feature of Poundbury is that both detached and terraced houses, shops and offices and workshops will knit closely together so that a simple ten-minute walk along its cobbled streets will enable the resident to reach any part of the village. At the heart of the first phase of the building is a square which will be surrounded by shops and offices. The square will also contain a 'market hall', which will also house a cafe and meeting room. Alongside the hall a familiar, 80 feet tall, church-like tower will be visible from all corners of the village. The village could become the envy of many city dwellers. Although its idealized top-down conception may fit uneasily with the real people who come to live there, it may be easier for existing neighbourhoods to capture the atmosphere and calm reassurance of village life.

The 'poor man's' 'bottom-up' Prince Charles of many an urban village is its church, residents' group, housing association, Development Trust, school and cluster of schools. These can become its strength and the engine which drives its development. It is not just the teacher, housing manager and voluntary sector professional who must be at the service of their 'clients and customers' in this way, but also the doctor, architect, accountant, indeed every professional whose energy is needed in the rebuilding of communities. The professional or social entrepreneur who consults, participates and is employed by local people becomes an appreciated part of the neighbourhood rather than a feared visitor from a different and more powerful one.

Refashioning democracy

The democratic system is supposed to enable people in neighbourhoods to freely choose their representatives and government. Yet, at most elections, the resident is confronted by two or three candidates chosen by the big parties and others who have no hope of election. The active, but diminishing, core of each party is always re-elected. Often, only the beginner and second raters are placed in unwinnable contests. If you live in a politically safe area you have no choice and if you are in an unwinnable area you can choose only between learners and failures.

Although there are notable exceptions, almost by definition politicians are principally concerned with gaining and keeping power in order to implement their policies from the top down. Often they are not interested in, or suited to, wielding direct influence within the neighbourhood or helping it to build itself up from ground level. Even those who see the point of such action often cannot spare the time to undertake it. As a result political parties do not do justice to the rich variety of practical circumstances which define life in neighbourhoods. So most people in each urban village are in effect disenfranchised. The point can be illustrated in Figure 17, below.

Only the activists within the circles A and B, within the wider community, C, are represented. The unwritten agenda of the wider community, D, is unseen by either party. This is perhaps why less than a third of the electorate vote in local elections. This means that councillors directly represent only around 15% of the electorate; the remaining 85% are

Figure 17: *Political parties and the community*

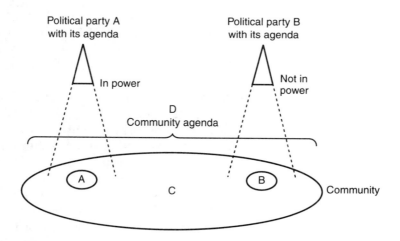

effectively disenfranchised. Their experience of local democracy is like a plausible confidence trick – it offers the illusion, but not the substance of choice and influence.

The urban village and the active citizen

It is not sufficient to devolve finances and managerial control out to schools and community agencies and for local authorities to become more customer sensitive as Henry Tam describes: parts of the political process itself must also be devolved. The emergent self-governing urban village needs its own non-party political voice and a degree of control over its own affairs if it is to fully emerge an identity of its own.

Parish Councils have a legal existence. Those rural villages which have retained these interesting forms of local democracy elect their own parish councillors to represent their own very local concerns. The Parish Council is able to levy a precept on the rate of one or two pence in the pound, which can give the parish councillors a useful income to spend as they and their constituents see fit. Most employ their own professional parish clerk who services and acts for the parish and its parish councillors.

Many people might respond far more positively to their own urban neighbourhood council or forum than to their party political councillor because they would see the immediate and positive results of their representations. Because most city council wards encompass at least three natural neighbourhoods, in place of one to three local councillors who must also relate to the whole city, there might emerge three sets of, say, fifteen neighbourhood forum representatives and people co-opted from local agencies such as schools, housing associations and Development Trusts. The neighbourhood officer or social entrepreneur could be funded either by a small precept on the rate, by pooling a part of the budget of the major local self-governing agencies or by being employed by the local Community Development Trust.

Some will wonder where so many active citizens might spring from to employ such a person. But it is relevant to point to the 10,000-strong population of the urban village of Balsall Heath, where the Community Development Trust operates with 50 volunteers who staff its various management boards. Some six residents' groups are attended by some two hundred people every month. The six schools' governing bodies meet termly and have various working committees. So they increase the number of active citizens by a factor of 6 times 15. If those who attend their church, temple and mosque councils or who patrol their street corners are included, the number of active citizens goes over the 1000 mark. So, to elect, say, twenty of these to represent the area and employ their own entrepreneur doesn't seem to be expecting too much. Yet, there is nothing unique about Balsall Heath: most neighbourhoods could become as lively if they were offered the serious possibility of excavating and improving the quality of life in their neighbourhood.

The involvement of so many people can and should be dignified by the local schools, their family centre and the local college engaging them in certificated Citizen Awareness courses. Indeed, with the help of cable and home computers, such a course could bring to life an open access neighbourhood college in which the whole community is enrolled. The point is not just an educational one. Modern versions of the Greek city state, in which all who wish to participate can do so, are no longer so fanciful, particularly when decisions are being made on local subjects where first-hand experience is so important.

The social entrepreneur and the new Town Hall

The neighbourhood officer's role might first be to help people to gain the confidence to formulate and express shared goals, to develop their own neighbourhood agenda. Second, it could be to help them to press these goals upon the city authorities and to ensure that they are acted upon. However, third, and more important, it should be possible for the forum to achieve many of its aims on its own with little more than passing reference to the town centre. With the help of its schools, housing associations and community development trusts, the neighbourhood forum would help to stimulate the social, economic and environmental development of the neighbourhood.

Although it is novel to the urban scene, the active citizen's neighbourhood forum, their entrepreneurial officer and those local voluntary and non-government institutions which relate and are accountable to them do not comprise an additional layer of government, which further complicates the organization of the democratic process. Rather, they take the place of significant parts of the previously over-intrusive city machine. As a consequence, the Town Hall can concentrate its efforts less on trying to run everything and thus failing to do anything well, but on enabling and resourcing others to achieve excellence.

Because so many of the tasks once undertaken by the Town Hall can readily and more effectively be discharged within each village, it is necessary to reduce its size and change the way it is organized. Most of the Town Hall's departments can be slimmed down or merged in order to meet new functions.

Old-style departments were organized in terms of specialist professional functions – education, social services, housing, etc. – as well as in pyramid-like hierarchies. This suited the needs of city wide planning, but it was of little benefit to neighbourhoods which recognize different boundaries and needs. It follows that a fresh, neighbourhood-sensitive, city department is needed which cuts across the city's old bureaucratic specialisms and planning areas. This new department must regard neighbourhoods as the basic building blocks from which towns are constructed. Instead of being organized segmentally and hierarchically this department would, therefore, subtend an array of sub-departments, one for each neighbourhood or cluster of neighbourhoods. These neighbourhood sub-departments would marshal and deploy the levers of local government to service and enhance the growth points of each area.

Because the aim of this new department is to boost the confidence of the individual, to see to it that others assist the developing child, and take part in the revitalization of neighbourhoods, it could be called the Neighbourhood Enterprise Department (NED). Once these new neighbourhood departments are devolved out to area offices in each neighbourhood they, in effect, become its new mini Town Hall.

The mini Town Hall would be the city's devolved top-down lever with which the bottom-up neighbourhood forum would liaise. It might be based in an extension of one of the village's schools, library, shopping centre or Trust and become one of its focal features. These proposals are not mere supposition. Hillingdon and Kent have merged several departments to create a new community-orientated one. Tower Hamlets has devolved most of its services. Braintree District Council has already implemented many of Henry Tam's suggestions, and John Stewart and Michael Clark at Birmingham University have written extensively about British examples of good practice. Recently, the DoE has challenged Manchester, Birmingham and London to become 'Cities of Pride'. It has asked them to define what they might look like in the years after the new millennium. The winds of change are blowing. As the dust which it stirs settles, it is possible to see what might replace the old pyramid-like Town Hall (Figure 18, page 144).

City governments are now multi-billion pound, complex organizations. They are impossibly larger than the ones with which Joseph Chamberlain could identify. It is not possible for voluntary councillors to manage such a modern organization efficiently. It needs time, devotion, confidence and an acquired expertise – otherwise the existing departments of full-time professional officers will follow their own course. High calibre, part-time or full-time city councillors are needed to steer a fresh course if sustainable Cities of Pride are to become more vital than the nation state and if new NED departments are to be refashioned and bent to the will of the community. So, it makes sense to pay the chairs of committees just as MPs are paid. Further, it makes sense to pay the Lord Mayor of each town. Instead of being largely ceremonial, the role of Lord Mayor should become more like that of the town's president. The office holder should be directly elected, not chosen by existing councillors on a political ticket.

There is scope for further experimentation and the evolution of new forms of participation and the most effective means by which such participation

Figure 18

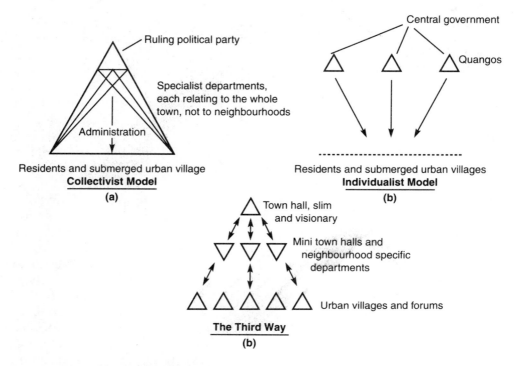

Ruling political party

Specialist departments, each relating to the whole town, not to neighbourhoods

Administration

Residents and submerged urban village
Collectivist Model
(a)

Central government

Quangos

Residents and submerged urban villages
Individualist Model
(b)

Town hall, slim and visionary

Mini town halls and neighbourhood specific departments

Urban villages and forums

The Third Way
(b)

Source: *Collectivist, Individualist and the Third Way Models. DEMOS (1994)*

can form dynamic partnerships with revitalized modes of representative democracy. Perhaps, as Stephen Thake has suggested, half a dozen authorities and/or neighbourhoods should form an alliance to pioneer the development of new partnerships between urban villages and other local authorities.

PERSPECTIVES FROM THE POLITICIANS

Paddy Ashdown – Gordon Brown – Alan Howarth

I. Paddy Ashdown

The philosophy of community politics has been central to my Party's thinking – and action – for over a quarter of a century now. Back in 1970 the Liberal Party formally adopted, as its *raison d'être*, the key tenet of community politics – that the whole point of politics is to help people in communities to take and use power themselves. I believe the social, economic and political changes in the twenty-five years since then have made the community politics approach not just necessary but essential. There is a real sense of dislocation in our society – and an urgent need for a bit of reconnection. Economic forces have become so global that people often feel completely powerless in the face of forces beyond their control. A less deferential, less hierarchical, less rule-bound society has brought greater insecurity and isolation, as well as the benefits of a more open society.

I begin with some observations on the situation in which we find ourselves. First, we live at a time of intense disillusionment with politics. This problem is not unique to Britain – witness the Canadian and American elections of 1994. But because our political system in Britain is so centralized, secretive and closed-off, I believe we are particularly ill-equipped to deal with it.

Second, look at our cities. Cities are places of extremes. For many people, they are great places to live and work. For many – well let's just say they could be a great deal better. Alongside concentrations of affluence and a huge range of facilities and opportunities, our cities also contain ghettos of poverty and powerlessness, decay and despair.

There are now two absolutely critical political tasks ahead of us. First, what John Biffen has called 'adjusting expectations' after a cosy era of what he dubbed 'growth and easy distribution'. The second task is to combat alienation by giving everyone a sense of a 'stake' in society's success. The task of overcoming alienation certainly does not make any easier the task of adjusting expectations. But what I believe *is* true is that people having power and responsibility in their own communities is critical to the success of both.

Unfortunately, our paternalistic political system has comprehensively failed to prepare the British people for this new era. Instead of fostering active citizens, our system sustains the British people in a passive political dependency.

National renewal and social cohesion can only come by turning our political system on its head by involving people in decision-making, binding people into difficult choices, and enabling people to take control of their own lives.

Look in particular at our cities and the message is the same. Our cities have massive potential. I am convinced they can be dynamic, supportive, prosperous places for the vast majority of the people who live there. But I am also convinced that the key to creating Cities of Pride does not lie in quangos, or consultants, or cosmetic solutions, but in putting power into the hands of local people and saying: 'This is your community – it's not up to me, it's up to you – so go for it!' The essence of community politics is saying: 'I'm not here to do things for you but to help you do things for yourself.' What I am talking about is not tinkering – it is a complete revolution in how we deal with regeneration and development.

The hard fact is that we will never overcome the problems of modern urban life – or release the potential that exists in our cities – with imposed, top-down solutions. In everything from planning to economic development, from environmental action to local decision-making – modern solutions must give power, responsibility and *ownership* to local communities.

In part, this means giving local councils more power and freedom to innovate and experiment. The centralization of power over the last fifteen years has completely undermined the local political experimentation that is vital for a healthy modern democracy – this must be reversed.

But decentralization of power should not stop at the Town Hall. Local government bureaucracies are too often remote, inefficient and insensitive to local needs. We should be turning these bureaucracies on their heads – taking services out to local neighbourhoods; devolving decision-making; handing power over to tenants, for example, not just for day-to-day running of their estates, but to decide how much money they want to spend on services and which services they want.

We should be turning councils inside out and transforming them into streamlined strategic and enabling authorities. Take schools: of course we need a strategic and accountable framework for local education – not least for reasons of efficiency – but within that framework schools should be given as much freedom as possible to develop in their own chosen ways. We should be harnessing new technology to enable schools to expand their role, not just as an education service, but as a development service for the whole community.

Like John Rennie, my vision of schools is not of building-based providers of 8.30 a.m. to 3.30 p.m. classes for 5- to 18-year-olds, but as round-the-clock centres of community education networks for the whole community.

Nothing has reinforced my belief in the huge regenerating potential of community power more than what I have seen, in concrete practical achievement, with my own eyes. Take the 'Planning for Real' scheme I saw in Brick Lane. As Joe Holyoak describes so well, through 'Planning for Real', architects are transformed from *experts* imposing ready-made solutions into *consultants*, helping local communities to create their *own* solutions. One woman who lived in Brick Lane said to me: 'Learning how to work with architects, reading their plans, designing our own community is the best higher education we have ever had.'

Of course, it's not just about bricks and mortar – it's all about building self-confidence and fostering pride in the local environment. The bottom line is that self-confidence and self-respect, involvement and control will do more to improve an area than any amount of money or experts with pre-planned solutions.

Or take crime. In Solihull in the West Midlands, you will find a Crime Reduction Programme, rooted in the community, bringing different groups together: young and old, schools, the police, the local council, parish councils, businesses, voluntary organizations – and really making an impact in preventing crime from happening. But the clear message from Ollie Goode, the co-ordinator, was this: 'If initiatives are to work, they have to come from the bottom up. Unless people feel ownership of what they do, they won't believe in it and it won't work.' There are no blueprints. That's the whole point. What we need is a ferment of experimentation on the ground. What we don't need is constant change from the government.

At the moment we see one 'urban initiative' launched after another. Every year the various pots of money are reorganized, the rules for getting to them are changed, and new teams are set up to co-ordinate activities. Around this plethora of quango-directed effort, a burgeoning industry of consultants has grown up to offer advice on ways round the Byzantine complexity of these 'initiatives'.

The whole problem is that this approach is essentially top down. Lasting solutions will come *only* from communities themselves. There is now an ever-expanding body of good practice, in Britain and abroad, in local government and in community development. We should be disseminating these ideas, showing people how they too can help themselves and then helping them to do the same.

Pass power down, let people experiment, give them effective support, and involve them, and we will begin to revitalize our local communities. To all the doubting Thomases, all I say is: 'Go and see for yourself. This isn't a theory any longer: it's hard, practical reality – and it's working.'

I want to conclude on an idea which Gordon, Frank, myself and all Opposition politicians should keep constantly in mind. The American elections in November 1994 did not just reflect a shift to the right. They also, and perhaps more importantly, reflected a shift towards an anti-political populism. There is now a real lack of faith in 'traditional' political solutions.

What worries me is that the easy 'anti-political' response to this disillu-sionment is atavistic and atomistic – a zero-sum individualism which undermines everything which most of us understand by 'society'. This route is not about expanding the Contented Society; it's about closing *off* the Contented Society behind barricades of barbed wire and private security guards. It's not about giving hope to the Excluded Society; it's about better protecting your individual life *from* the Excluded Society. This, for me, is a frightening prospect. The message for those of us who reject that approach should be obvious. People have lost faith in traditional political solutions. We'd better offer something better – or someone else will pretty soon begin to offer something much worse.

We should not be thinking about the Contented Society or the Excluded Society – we should be trying to build a *Stakeholder* Society in which everyone has a stake in society and the power to act to change their lives for the better. I believe the community is the cornerstone of a positive new approach to replace exhausted political solutions.

Therefore we must reinvigorate the sense of community:

- as a framework in which people understand their responsibilities to each other;
- as the means with which people can take control of their own lives;
- as a vehicle for practical action, which solves problems.

II. Gordon Brown

I start from the optimistic view of human nature which holds that people are co-operative as well as competitive, that we are interdependent as well as dependent. I start from the view that the dividing line is between those who see Britain simply as a market place of buyers and sellers competing with each other, vying with each other for preference, as against Britain as a community of citizens with shared values, common destinies, linked purposes and mutual needs. I believe that is the true dividing line in our society today. So, what I want to do here is to build on the idea of community, putting into practice many of the ideas that we have talked about in theory.

I want to start from what I think is the fundamental problem that we are all trying to grapple with, both as politicians and people in all different walks of community life. Basically, there have been four turning points in British politics this century, that have shifted the relationship between the individual, community and government.

First, before 1945, the state did little. The community operated through voluntary organizations, charitable aid and mutual societies; but it could not do enough to deal with both the poverty and lack of opportunity in our society. Second, 1945 brought a new settlement between individual, community and state. The welfare state, the creation of the health service and the guarantee of employment was seen by millions of people as a deliverance from the problems that we faced in the 1930s and before that.

Gradually, however, that new relationship between individual and community and state started to break down. The individual was to be guaranteed social security and opportunity through the workings of a benevolent state. But what actually happened, and we all know it happened locally as well as nationally, is that the state somehow became a substitute for the community rather than an extension of it.

So we had great national industries that were remote both from the workforce and the consumers. We had great institutions like the health service that gradually moved further and further away from both patients and the professionals who were working in it. We had great demands for benevolent administration but we did not have the devolution of power in Scotland and Wales and to the other regions of England that people were seeking. Gradually the productive relationship between individual, community and state became the state identified with the community and a substitute for it. This became unacceptable to people.

Third, we then had the making of a new relationship between individual, community and state and that happened around 1979. Mrs Thatcher exploited the widely held perception that there was too much bureaucracy, too much collectivism, that the state had actually failed. Indeed, at worst, the state was a substitute for community.

Her perspective, which became the common view during the 1980s, was that somehow the individual could and should succeed on his or her own, independent of activity by the community and the state. So, the state was withdrawn from activities in life that previously were guaranteed in the 1945 settlement.

At the same time, charities and voluntary organizations were asked to take on responsibilities hitherto taken on by government, but there was not the flowering of community life that should have arisen from it. Indeed, the famous remark that there is no such thing as society, gave some the view that the new relationship was individuals on their own without the community and state working with them.

Fourth, I now believe we are actually at a new turning-point in our affairs. It's nothing to do with political party support or with which particular leaders are popular at this particular moment. This new relationship between individual, community and state accepts the failings of both previous relationships, between 1945 and 1979, and between 1979 and 1994. People again want to build a new settlement where individuals are recognized as the decision-makers in their own lives and where community is actually at work in practice through voluntary organizations, mutual aid societies, voluntary and community activity, and where government is seen not as a substitute for these things but as a facilitator.

I came into politics from community action and not the other way round. But the problem for those of us who have supported the idea of community is that we are living in a changing world where five things have happened.

First, we have seen the globalization of the economy which creates a new world of work in which no one is guaranteed a living. Second, we see a new world of the family where marriages break down at a far faster rate than ever before and there are so many 'atomized units' in society who feel that they owe obligations to no one. Third, the state has come to be seen by many people as a vested interest.

Fourth, is the problem of geographical and social immobility. Undoubtedly the old territorial loyalties of the past, the kinship and the neighbourhood, are coming under strain. Fifth, people's aspirations are far greater and wider and broader than they were before, and that is particularly true of women who are wanting opportunities to realize their potential, and a welfare state and an employment system that is capable of helping them to realize their aims.

People now want to be decision-makers in their own right, to make decisions that previously were made by organizations on their behalf. At the same time, changing mobility structures in our society mean that community cannot be the same as it was before.

The right-wing view has been to suggest that because these changes are happening, community can never exist in any form in any significant way again. It seems to me that we should come back to the basic principle of community and build from there. And the basic principle of community is mutuality, it is the recognition of interdependence. You cannot begin a new politics in this country and reinvent government until you recognize that you must reconstruct this idea of community and build an awareness amongst people of interdependence, until community and loyalties are stimulated and expanded and until we have policies that put the theory of community action into practice.

We need not be pessimistic. Of course there is social disintegration, of course there is a breakdown in law and order, of course people feel that there is an endemic loneliness in our society and that there is indifference to the social problems that people face. But at the same time, I think people increasingly recognize that individuals can only succeed as part of a community and that we have got to rebuild the sense of interdependence. I think we now recognize that the biggest problems that we face as a community, the breakdown of law and order, unfairness, pollution, congestion and the lack of investment in education for our future can no longer be addressed by either individuals acting on their own or by the pursuit of privatization or free-market forces. They can only be addressed by us working together as a community and trying to solve these problems together.

So, I suggest that it is time for a new relationship between individual, community and state. This relationship recognizes that individuals are empowered through the actions of the community. The state is not a substitute for community but must be seen as a facilitator, a partner, a catalyst. That is, we no longer take the one-dimensional view of government 'top-down' services provided in a hierarchical way.

The question then becomes: How do we apply these ideas in practice to a new world? First, there's got to be major constitutional change. It is not just the Bill of Rights that safeguards individuals against entrenched interests, and it is not just the reform of the House of Lords, necessary though that is, for these are reforms at the centre. It must also be our policy to devolve power as a matter of principle whenever it is possible. I don't just mean devolution to Scotland and Wales and to the Regions. It must entail local government looking at how it can devolve its services and the management of them to a local neighbourhood level. So the principle of any new constitutional settlement must be to devolve power wherever possible to make a reality of community action so that we can engage problems by working together collectively as a community.

The second area where there has got to be a change is in what has become the quango state. It is not right that 50,000 appointees, who were neither elected nor drawn from community organizations in any way whatsoever, are spending 20% of public money on our behalf. There are more unelected people in big bodies making decisions than are elected. So, the initial task of government in relation to quangos is to end the secrecy, to make a bonfire of quangos wherever possible and to have democracy restored.

The third area of change is in the area of policy itself. It is no good talking about constitutional settlements if you cannot apply the principles to the everyday decision-making that affects education, health, law and order and the organization of services in your community. There is no space to describe how my ideas affect every particular service. So, let me take as an example, the health service.

It seems to me it is a matter of principle that the solution to many of our health problems is to involve people in discussing, debating and deciding their own solutions. Therefore, greater democratization of the health service, greater community involvement, greater emphasis on preventative medicine must be a principle that governs any approach to policy.

As far as law and order is concerned we know that the 'top-down' approach, simply giving heavy sentences, cannot in itself work unless there is a community determination to take action that both exposes those who are criminals and deals with causes of crime. A partnership between local communities, the police and the professionals in each area is absolutely essential if the problems of crime are to be dealt with. Tony Blair has put forward a number of exciting proposals which have caught the imagination.

As far as education is concerned, I too agree with John Rennie: the school and the college must be at the hub of the community. Further, the application of these principles of community to education, helped by technology, opens up enormous opportunities to us. We can now pioneer new public institutions in education that give people the chance to fulfil their potential.

In the new world of satellite and cable technology, it is possible to link home to school; it is also possible to link homes and neighbourhoods to colleges and universities. The young and adults who are the most disadvantaged can be linked to the best teachers in the world, and the new technology can give communities more power to make decisions about their education system.

In the 1960s we had a new initiative in education: we formed the Open University and used television technology to bring education to people's homes; this gave thousands of people the chance of university education who otherwise would have missed out. So, also, in the 1990s it is possible to use cable, satellite and the new information highways to open up new opportunities for people in the home and in the workplaces of this country. It is possible to get education at any level by linking schools, colleges, universities and homes in a new educational revolution. The University for Industry that I have set out ideas to implement, is one way to again make connections between home, school, college and university. I look forward to further discussion on how this educational revolution can move forward, applying these principles of community to the practice of education.

If we are to apply the principles of community helping individuals to realize their potential, then there has got to be a revolution in the workplace as well, a recognition that the future of our economy depends on us being able to liberate individual potential through tackling vested interests that lie in our way, and giving people the opportunity to have the best chance of the highest living standards and earning power, as well as to make a contribution to the development of the community. I think companies must now recognize that their great asset is not capital, which can be bought anywhere, but skills. It is ironic that the whole of company organization is built around the power of capital rather than on allowing people to be members of the firm, decision-makers in the process of economic and industrial changes.

At the same time, we must tackle a whole series of vested interests that hold people back. I applaud Birmingham for the many advances that have been made in trying to develop community banking, but I think that we can go further. We can learn from the Community Reinvestment Act in the States that banks and people in the community can get together to create local banking services in the poorest areas of our country. At the same time banks and financial institutions are in a position to give people the resources to start businesses, to be self-employed, for third-sector organizations to work, and for community business to flourish. This seems to me to be crucial in the reform of the relationship between the financial institutions and the economic system as a whole.

The final area I want to discuss is unemployment – the biggest problem that we face as a community. Out of the alienation that is caused by the lack of jobs is bred disillusionment and crime. I want to propose a number of measures for dealing with unemployment that are at a national level.

I believe that we have got to give new powers and responsibilities to community organizations, third-sector groups and community businesses to employ people who are long-term unemployed in their own communities as a means by which we help the process of industrial regeneration. This is one of a number of proposals that I want to put forward to deal with long-term unemployment and particularly to deal with youth employment.

I want to release capital receipts to let local authorities build and encourage small businesses by a number of measures. At the same time, an energy efficiency scheme that allows us to insulate homes and offices in part of the country would be partly paid for by any windfall tax on the huge excess profits made by the privatized utilities.

There is one other measure I think we should look at: we need an environmental task force for young people. The Americans formed the peace corps, which galvanized a whole generation of young people. Now, in the 1990s, it is in my view possible to build on a whole series of voluntary initiatives that are already taking place and create an environmental or green corps for young people. We could form a national community service that is open to all young people, not exclusively to the unemployed, but which is open to people with qualifications and with no qualifications; it would involve not just service in Britain but have an avenue for environmental work overseas as well. In time it could be expanded beyond Britain and involve the rest of the European Community. This seems to me a practical realization of the principles of community in action without stepping across a number of initiatives that are already taking place.

The problems that we face are huge and sometimes overbearing – the breakdown of law and order, the disintegration of communities, high unemployment, pollution, a sense of unfairness in our society, a sense that things have gone wrong, that they cannot any longer be solved other than by people working together as a community. This demands that we apply the new relationship between individual, community and government to the new challenges that we have ahead. But even then, it requires that there is a recognition by people that we are in this together, that we are a community and not simply a set of markets, that we succeed when we work together.

An unknown American described this idea of interdependence better than any other. He wrote that: 'It is not the invisible hand that determines how our society works and will continue to work in the future. Society depends on the hands of others. It is the hands of others that grow the food we eat, who sew the clothes we wear, who build the homes we inhabit. It is the hands of others who tend us when we are sick and who raise us up when we fall. It is the hands of others who lift us first from the cradle and then more or less into the grave.' It is this notion of interdependence and mutuality which is at the centre of a new move forward in both our politics and community life.

III. Alan Howarth

We live in a society of increasing insecurity. National governments are in important respects impotent as the information technology revolution and the vastly powerful global markets it has created transform our ways of living. Some 59% of men aged between 55 and 64 are now out of employment, compared to 8% in 1977. How can we reconcile economic energy with solidarity and social cohesion? There is intense pressure on welfare budgets. It is not just low-income workers who live with casualization and insecurity, but people far up the income scale. To our shame, the poorest 10% of households have not shared in the overall growth of the nation's wealth. Unemployment and insecurity are particularly acute in deprived urban areas, sadly including the Sparkbrook, Nechells, Aston, Ladywood and Handsworth areas of Birmingham. Is Marx about to be proved right after all, with widening inequality polarizing and destabilizing our society? Or will deprived areas just stagnate in listlessness? Neither outcome is acceptable. And, as creative initiatives have already shown in Birmingham and other cities, neither need occur.

Of course there are huge problems, against which the individual feels, and often is, powerless. Government certainly has no sure answers. But the contradictions in our society are not leading us inexorably to disintegration: our resources of community are not exhausted.

How then can national politicians help people to create strong, self-reliant communities? 'I'm from the government, I'm here to help you.' Great lie, or new reality?

To start with, national politicians can resolve that 'community' should be more than a euphemism. Community Charge, Care in the Community, European Community and, most cynically, Building Stable Communities – these have not helped give community a good name. Appreciation of the vital importance of community, in a worthwhile sense of the word, is, however, growing across the political spectrum. The deficiencies of the conventional ideologies – Labour's excessive faith in big government, Conservatives' in the individual – are increasingly recognized by the parties themselves. We all see more clearly now that people need support as social beings. Public policy should sustain, in Amitai Etzioni's phrase, a community of communities. Our social ecology, like our natural environment, is fragile and needs nurturing.

Amiable sentiments alone butter no parsnips, however. Nor will lip-service to community be easy for politicians to translate into consistent and thoroughgoing practice, for that requires humility, and in most politicians there are more than average quotas of vanity and desire for power. Neither politicians nor bureaucrats are very good at sharing, and that too is implied by communitarianism. The radicalism that we need is not the radicalism that insists on imposing our superior wisdom and turning other people's lives upside down, but radical change to politics itself. It seems, all things considered, unlikely that we are entering a new age of political ecumenism but some of the old antagonisms of left and right are now manifestly irrelevant, and we may at least be able to agree that the job of politicians is to support and empower people in their communities and that leadership involves partnership.

Partnership is another cliché but we must now allow it to be drained of meaning. So often when public services fail it is because responsibility has collapsed into the gaps between organizations. It is the people who most need help who suffer from demarcation disputes between departments and between levels of government. Government, centrally and locally, is too fragmented, where it needs to be holistic.

For example, for reasons that must have seemed compelling, a Conservative Government split up the DHSS into a Department of Health and a Department of Social Security. A Labour Government had previously removed responsibility for health from local authorities, leaving them as social services authorities. We now see health authorities busy trying to transfer responsibility for the care of the long-term sick to social services. The policies and practices of social services authorities, health authorities and housing authorities as well need to be integrated for care in the community. Rightly the government has enjoined on them a shared obligation to assess and provide for the care needs of the individual; but the structure which governments have created makes it difficult for them to do so. Some of the agencies are elective, some are appointed: they are not physically coterminous – they have varying and conflicting priorities, and have different budgets and different sources of finance.

We must not allow such factors to prevent, and nothing in the rules which Whitehall makes must impede, the integration of services and the cross-fertilization of activities. I have in mind, for instance, the development of schools as family centres which Dick Atkinson so excitingly envisages in *The Common Sense of Community*.[1]

If government more often established task-related budgets rather than departmental budgets it would help. It happens to an extent: City Challenge has encouraged local authorities to take the lead in mobilizing all the resources of their communities to work together in agreed purposes. The Single Regeneration Budget is a very large-scale initiative in this direction. We need to work more closely with integrated budgets on well-defined, shared tasks.

Inter-departmental ministerial groups convene – like those on which I served on drug abuse and energy conservation – but so long as they do not have integrated budgets of their own their efforts are less effective than they could be. The same too commonly happens in local government. Departments working with disparate budgets are more prone to be narrow-visioned, possessive and unco-operative when they're flush, and to shuffle off their responsibilities when the money runs short.

The Archbishop of Canterbury, in his recent address on Faith, Hope and

Love in an Insecure Society, observed that fragmentation and discontinuity characterize our insecure world. Urban policy has been no exception. Urban Programme, Inner Area Programme, Enterprise Zones, Urban Development Agencies, Urban Development Corporations, Estate Action, the Manpower Services Commission, the Training Commission, the Training Agency, Training and Enterprise Councils and the Training, Enterprise and Education Directorate have all come and gone, or not gone yet.

When I was involved as a Minister with our programme intended to regenerate East Birmingham, Heartlands drew on City Grant, Estate Action, Housing Association Grant, Industrial Improvement Area Grants, DTI Transport Grant, Urban Programme, Task Force and TEC programmes, Birmingham City Council discretionary funding (numerous departments and sub-heads there), European Regional Development Fund and private sector investment. I used to ask myself, as George Orwell asked in *England Your England*: 'How can we make a pattern out of all this muddle?' The Single Regeneration Budget needs to provide an important part of this answer.

Improved coherence in government needs to be matched by increased decentralization: this has already been occurring. Next Steps Agencies and quangos are exercising power delegated from Whitehall in a large number of fields, as we well know. The unsatisfactory aspects of these arrangements are fragmentation, lack of transparency and lack of adequate accountability. Accountability to the consumer, a merit in itself, is not a satisfactory substitute for accountability to the citizen. In *The Governance Gap* John Plummer[2] has described how quangos look toward central government for terms of reference and, grudgingly, audit, but do not look around them to see how they should relate to their fellow quangos and do not look down, so to speak, to respond to the views and wishes of the public they exist to serve.

Since World War II central government, of both parties, has reduced the scope and autonomy of local government. The driving force, at least since the mid-1970s, has been the Treasury, and the greatest assertion of central government power has been capping. I want to see a restoration of the authority of local government. Belief in pluralism and respect of local tradition and continuity are, I was brought up to think, Tory values. A so-called 'civic' Conservatism that systematically outflanks and atrophies local government is, literally, a nonsense. I regard elective local government as a key expression of community and I believe that local politics can, potentially, forge and sustain local community.

There are four specific proposals that I would like to make. First, capping should be ended. Local authorities should be accountable to their communities for the revenue that they raise and the services they provide. Centrally imposed limits on local authority borrowing are necessary for macro-economic policy purposes, but existing fiduciary and audit requirements and the accountability provided through the Council Tax, at any rate where there are annual elections, are sufficient safeguards against excessive current expenditure. Second, the business rate – nationalized by a Conservative Government – should be restored to local authorities. That would help to strengthen the links between local authorities and their business communities. Third, where possible, quangos should be made locally accountable. That must include transparency in appointments and procedures, at the least; councillors appointed to quangos; elective quangos; and a review of quango functions to see which could be transferred to local government.

Finally, is it not time at least to consider whether a power of general competence should be vested in local government? Local government's powers derive, constitutionally, from statute. In Britain, by contrast to other European countries, local authorities exercise only those powers specifically allowed to them. Parliament should be more generous in its concept of local democracy. Should not local authorities be free to undertake such activities as they choose which Parliament has not specifically debarred?

The condition for these reforms must, however, be that local authorities similarly decentralize. I also want local government to renew itself. Centralized, bureaucratic, overbearing local government will not meet the needs of communities. Unitary local authorities have much to be said for them, but not monopolistic local authorities.

Local government should decentralize its own administration and service delivery. It should foster varieties of local fora and neighbourhood compacts. It should mobilize, support and orchestrate a wide variety of agencies: public, voluntary and commercial. It should recognize that the gentleman in the Town Hall really does not know best, any more than the gentleman in Whitehall. Objectives will be better identified, and gain understanding and willing assent, when there has been not just consultation but full involvement by local people in decision-making. The principle of subsidiarity, indeed, must be carried right through. Decisions, allocation of resources and accountability should be at the lowest practicable level.

Politicians and officials will not infrequently help best simply by letting go; after all, we have imposed so many bad ideas in the past. We have planned to separate work and living. We have spent huge sums facilitating people to travel away from city centres and live outside them. We have bulldozed and rebuilt whole areas, only then to realize that our actions have traumatized if not shattered local communities.

Communities, and the communitarian ethos, cannot be imposed: genuine communities are made by their own members. Politicians from outside can and must help them, with sensitivity, forbearance and patience. We need not doubt the will and tenacity of human beings in making communities. Richard Hoggart[3] described, with passionate sympathy, in *The Uses of Literacy*, the strong neighbourhood communities and culture originally formed in the turmoil of the Industrial Revolution and thriving socially even amid material poverty. We see around us today a wealth of voluntary, public-spirited and indeed, convivial activity. Our job as politicians is to support its development, with the resources of tact, expertise and finance at our disposal.

One crucial way in which central government can help is to allow long enough timescales for these strategies. It takes time to build local capacity and confidence, where they are lacking. It takes time for projects to fulfil themselves. Economic recessions wreak appalling damage to fragile communities. The Treasury hates to look beyond the end of its nose. But if there is all-party agreement that support for communities on this kind of pattern is appropriate and that deprived areas deserve our first consideration, there is no reason why central and local government should not make ten-year commitments. The City Pride project is, I'm glad to say, predicated on these assumptions.

I have dwelt on central government's relationship with communities by way of its relationship with local government. Space does not allow me to comment, as I would like to have done, on government support for business. The Tomorrow's Company project seeks to redefine the social responsibility of companies, in their best business interest, to take fully into account their relations with a range of stakeholders, beyond the shareholder. This will need central government's endorsement in a remodelling of company law. Nor have I been able to dwell on central government's relations with the voluntary sector: I will only suggest that the best contracts are negotiated rather than imposed and that we should beware the ethical minimalism of contract culture. I would like to have considered the implications for national policy of the need for schools to educate young people better for relationships and citizenship and the Changemakers scheme, to involve young people more responsibly in the lives of their communities, which some Birmingham schools are exploring.

I shall leave you only with those hints. Communitarianism may change our politics – I hope it will. But the deeper value of communitarianism is that it does not depend upon government.

CONCLUSION

Dick Atkinson

The style of organization and culture of the public, private and third sectors are changing from ones they acquired in industrial society to ones appropriate to post-industrial society; but they are changing at different speeds and with differing degrees of understanding and appreciation.

After two hundred years of service to the industrial era, the mine and mill are closed and empty. Perhaps it is easy to accept the radical transformation which is under way because we can still see these physical relics of a bygone age and, alongside them in sharp contrast, the gleaming high-tech office of the new age. But it is also important to recognize that the nature of business organizations has also changed and that the style of organization in the public and third sector is similarly in the middle of a quantum change. However, unless we act as midwife to this change, the old style of organization will, like the old buildings, stand obstinately in the way of post-industrial economic, social and political recovery and progress.

The private sector

In his book, *The Age of Unreason*, Charles Handy[4] describes the typical old industrial business as being organized like a pyramid, with the managers at the apex and the workforce, who receive and obey orders, at the base. Once, the educated elite who staffed head office might have been thrusting and entrepreneurial in spirit and attitude. Over time, however, they became complacent, immune to change, and rule-bound. Compared with their competitors in America and Japan they became uncompetitive. As mill and mine closed and the high-tech office became a possibility, industrial concerns faced collapse unless they were prepared to undergo dramatic changes in form, attitude and product.

From being shaped like a pyramid, those companies which bravely underwent this change came to resemble a maypole, with a slim, charismatic, head office. The few senior managers who now occupy the new high-tech head office devolve much of the day-to-day decision-taking process to semi-autonomous units who thus hold the ribbons of the maypole. This new 'workforce' has a similar stake and say in the enterprise as those at the apex. The modern firm which has made these essential but painful changes is characterized by key features:

- It has undone the cumbersome rules and regulations of its previously large head office. It has written innovation into its new *modus operandi*.
- It employs fresh, visionary, senior managers and often deploys these out to a carefully redesigned, equally high-tech, factory floor in order to lead small, semi- or fully autonomous teams of enthusiastic staff.
- It expects these teams to take the initiative and tell head office how to resource them rather than to await orders.
- In the place of a once dependent, uneducated workforce, it employs fewer, but educated, skilled and self-motivating people who work 'with' not 'for' senior managers. It believes in 'workers control', except that the modern worker works by brain as well as by hand and is, in part, a manager and, often, a shareholder.
- Because the customer is seen as sovereign, great efforts are made to achieve a consistently high quality product and a socially and environmentally clean method of production.

Unlike the pyramid, the maypole is not bound together by traditional authority, rules and orders but by a common set of ideas and values which motivate all who associate together to form the company. And, within each part of the company, the aim is to foster self-reliance, autonomy and responsibility. The distinction between the pyramid and the maypole is pictured in Figure 19, below.

Clearly many businesses do not live up to this new post-industrial ideal. Many remain hierarchical, slow to adapt and most maintain tight control over some parameters, particularly finance. But the ideal is now widely

Figure 19

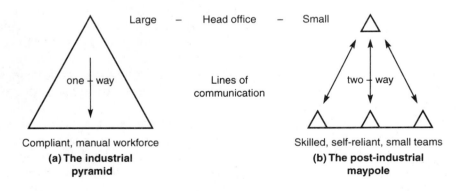

Large   –   Head office   –   Small

Lines of communication

one — way   two — way

Compliant, manual workforce   Skilled, self-reliant, small teams

(a) The industrial pyramid   **(b) The post-industrial maypole**

accepted. It has obvious implications for the way the public and third sectors are managed and related to each other.

The public sector

At first only private-sector organizations were obliged to move from A to B of Figure 18 by competition in the market place, new technology and new ideas. By contrast, public-sector organizations were slow to follow suit. They were protected from customer and community dissatisfaction by virtue of being public, one size fits all monopolies. Because they were subsidized by people as taxpayers through the state and not paid for directly by people as customers, they could afford to remain complacent, ineffective and ignore the needs of their dependent customers.

Gradually, however, governments have been forced to realize that they could not allow this antiquated situation to prevail; this is because modern customers of the public sector have become more choosy. Schooled by the range of high quality products of an effective private sector, they expect more than the standard national health pair of specs and require a more diverse and appropriate education than the standardized comprehensive education system could provide. Further, the welfare state has become so expensive that it is almost impossible for governments to afford. Necessity being the mother of invention, governments now ask if there are other ways of providing public services. They ask if new approaches offer both a better quality and cost-effective product. Perhaps the style and technique of the modern private sector can help?

The shift to new forms of government agency has been taking place across the developed world for some time. Many countries in Europe already have complex arrangements mixing government purchase of services and their provision by smaller voluntary, self-governing bodies, often associated with the church. New Zealand and Australia have also seen radical experiments in government. In their book, *Reinventing Government*, Osborn and Gaebler[5] have synthesized many of these experiences. They show how the collectivist, pyramid-like, governments of the industrial age came to both 'steer and row'. That is, governments tried both to set aims for their public agencies to follow and also to run those agencies themselves. In attempting to perform both tasks, governments came to leave the productive potential of most people out of their equation. Partly because of this, they also failed to perform either task very well. The increasingly sophisticated voter (customer) grew ever more restless and dissatisfied.

Both central and local government have begun to learn that to be effective they must slough off the agencies and services which they have attempted to provide for people and instead enable independent initiative to flourish. Such initiative can take the form of either private enterprise or publicly funded self-governing agencies, such as housing associations, schools and Development Trusts. Delegating the rowing function to such autonomous agencies does not entail 'privatization'. It merely means giving the initiative and the finances for the provision of government-approved services to those publicly and privately funded self-governing agencies which have the incentive to deliver a good product to the specifications which government lays down.

Government may delegate the task of rowing. But, at the behest of the customer, it must choose which services are required and to what quality, and it must then raise the taxes to pay for them. That is, it can't delegate the public task of 'governance'. This is the special, irreducible, function of government. It must set the style and shape of its town or country. Once freed from the impossible task of rowing, a slimmer, higher-minded government can concentrate on the job which only it can do, that of reflecting, co-ordinating and steering the hopes, aspirations and priorities of self-reliant citizens and self-governing and public agencies.

Old, industrially derived notions of government suggest to the left that more and more government agencies are needed and, to the right, that government should be rolled back completely, that all services and agencies should be 'privatized'. The one seeks to steer and row more vigorously, the other to do neither. Both attitudes miss the point. Stuck in the rut of industrial society, their advocates bedevil and confuse the debate about how to help the public sector to make the most effective transition from pyramid to maypole. For post-industrial forms of organization and the culture of the maypole require neither more nor less government, but a different kind of administration and thus a different kind of public agency.

The implications are dramatic and twofold. First, the quality of charity within the third sector has to be cut free from its industrially derived culture of dependence on the pyramid of local and central government and pulled into the self-reliant culture of the maypole. Second, the emerging vigorous third sector can only function effectively if it develops a new participatory relationship with a refocused public sector which has jettisoned its 'doing' role in favour of an 'enabling' one.

The third sector

The horrors of the dark satanic mill and mine encouraged people to ask the state to take on the main responsibilities for care and welfare. As it grew from small beginnings to become more powerful, representative democracy came to see self-reliance and charity as at best peripheral and, at worst, demeaning to the recipient. Thus, local and central government expanded to influence most areas of life until little stood between the individual and the state.

The unintended, destructive consequences of these developments were not at first apparent. Yet gradually they caused the state to take on from family, neighbourhood and church the responsibility for the care of others and stifle people's common impulse to take control of and shape their own lives. The creation of pyramid-like state monopolies in education, housing, planning and other walks of life not only produced a poor specialist product, it also took away from neighbourhoods their sense of self-reliance, ownership and purpose. For some time it has been apparent to people working in the third sector that a move from the pyramid to the maypole-like method of organization and culture is overdue.

The vital qualities of independence and self-reliance needed to help the third sector to thrive in the developed world were admirably defined twenty years ago by Erich Schumacher[6] in his book, *Small is Beautiful* which was addressed to those seeking to help the underdeveloped world. Although he was writing about how dependent peoples in Third World countries might become independent, his words are vitally relevant to large swaths of urban life in this country. He wrote:

The best aid to give is intellectual aid, a gift of useful knowledge. . . . Nothing becomes truly 'one's own' except on the basis of some genuine effort or sacrifice. . . . Give a man a fish as the saying goes, and you help him a little bit for a very short while; teach him the art of fishing, and he can help himself for all his life. On a higher level: supply him with fishing tackle; this will cost you a good deal of money, and the result remains doubtful; but even if fruitful, the man's continuing livelihood will still be dependent upon you for replacements. But, teach him to make his own fishing tackle and you have helped him to become not only self-supporting, but also self-reliant and independent.

Development Trusts, Planning for Real exercises, and social entrepreneurs are three means by which the third sector can build its own fishing tackle and regain a sense of pride. Self-governing housing associations and community schools are others. Proper training and funding for a new wave of social entrepreneurs are urgently needed to begin to bind together and make sense of these otherwise separate agencies and initiatives.

But such initiatives cannot blossom unless the existing mode of representative democracy is amended to include the vital new function of participation. One way of doing this is to form non-party political urban village forums, accountable to local people, which have real powers and can get things done. A newly emergent and strong third sector cannot function effectively unless the energies and style of the public sector and, in particular, the political parties and government are reinvented.

While the process of forming a new participatory relationship between the third and public sectors has begun, many do not yet understand the need for it or its far-reaching implications. We teeter in no-man's-land, pulled back by the old and beckoned forward by the new.

Participation and representation – responsibility and value

The new participatory relationship between the sectors can be glimpsed by contrasting it with the exercise of authority within the pyramid by those at the apex. They expected their dependent workforce to respect and obey their command whether they agreed with it or not. Authority passed down the line, not up it. Such a hierarchical system could be relied upon as long as those at the apex 'had enough information to take reasonable decisions which those at the bottom could not query or improve upon; as long as people worked with their hands and not their brains; as long as there were mass, undiscriminating markets; as long as people had similar needs'.[7]

But once trade unions, schools and new forms of communication helped people to ask awkward questions, the stability of this system was undermined: it became open to conflict and issues of class. Those at the bottom of the pyramid demanded rights of redress and, by degrees, those at the top conceded them in order to retain overall control. Society and the political process became a divided and adversarial stalemate.

In sharp contrast, those at the head of the maypole have a quite different kind of relationship with their self-governing ribbon-holders. This relationship depends not on orders but on the charisma, vision and values of enlightened leaders. It depends on their vision being understood, shared and reinforced by all who work within the agency. The strength of the organization thus depends on a set of voluntary and individual choices which interlock because they are guided by a common value. Authority and decisions pass in two directions, both up and down, in a fresh partnership which is sealed by the sense of responsibility which arises from mutual dependence and a shared value.

It is not sufficient to say that the pendulum must swing back from a relativistic, rights-orientated and divided society to one which is drawn together by a post-industrial sense of responsibility and shared values. In today's less deferential society the sense of responsibility, obligation and harmony which flow from shared values cannot be just asserted or taken for granted. In today's maypole, they have to be proved and won afresh. This means that a new vocabulary as well as a new vision appropriate to the modern age are needed if the maypole is to gain ascendancy within and between the public and third sectors and not just within the private one. We must get used to the language of family, community, participation, responsibility, obligation, duty, value and morality. Such terms and styles of thinking have always made common sense to many ordinary people. It is time that they came to be similarly accepted by politicians and that the gap between the ordinary person and the political parties was closed.

The reforms and vocabulary suggested in this book represent no more of an attack upon government than John Harvey-Jones'[8] attempts to give the kiss of life to failing businesses signifies an attack upon them. On the contrary, they could rescue the political process from decades of incipient inertia and popular resentment and herald a new era of acceptance and appreciation.

It is easy for defenders of the status quo to forget that the existing form of Town Hall and Whitehall democracy has already undergone many profound changes. Just two centuries ago, Tom Paine and others fought for the rights of man. In this century women had to chain themselves to the railings and staff the munitions factories in World War I to gain the vote. Full adult suffrage only became a reality after World War II.

Democracy has evolved and must continue to keep pace with the times. The modernizers within each of the three parties are aware of this, though they run the risk of being distracted by those colleagues who cannot escape the confines of traditional thinking about collectivities and rights and who cling to outmoded ways of wielding the levers of power. So, the modernizers as well as the third sector need every encouragement and help if their views are to prevail and the political process is to work with the grain of life rather than against it.

This help can come from at least four sources:

First, necessity is a great educator. As time goes by, and the voter becomes more and more sophisticated, it is less and less easy for the traditionalist to win power. Only politicians and parties which move with the times and offer 'customer service' stand a real chance of being elected.

Second, the better organized and more confident the third sector becomes, the more it will become impossible for the parties to ignore its unique ability to help neighbourhoods and community to develop.

Third, bold and bright politicians in each of the parties must continue to speak out and help to form a modern consensus.

Fourth, the independent community network which began to emerge during and after the Birmingham conference can provide the impetus for further experimentation, dissemination, reform and progress. It can and should become a kind of third sector, community development, academy of the airwaves which helps all existing networks to become more effective at identifying and presenting good practice, good ideas and policies at both the local and national levels.

When Charles Handy took the platform to summarize and close the Birmingham Cities of Pride Conference he said to the four hundred delegates: 'We started this morning with an anticipatory buzz. As the day progressed this buzz became more distinct and enveloping. Now it has reached a crescendo. Clearly, something special has happened today. It's audible and it's compelling. Others should, and no doubt will, hear it.'

In the days and weeks after the conference, I have indeed heard the same excited buzz arising from meetings in each of the four corners of the land. Just a few months ago, let alone years ago, it would have been impossible to detect such a sound even with the most finely tuned hearing aid. Until recently, the third-sector voice was too weak and discordant to rouse an echo, let alone a movement in the political system.

Now, it is not only possible to detect the voice of the third sector and hear the public and private sectors respond to it, it is impossible to ignore. It would seem that its moment has come. Can it truly rise to the occasion and assist with the rebuilding of community and the refocusing of government to create Cities of Pride?

Notes and references

1. DEMOS (1994) *The Common Sense of Community*. London.
2. Plummer, J. (1994) *The Governance Gap: Quangos and Accountability*. The Joseph Rowntree Foundation.
3. Hoggart, R. (1957) *The Uses of Literacy*. London: Pelican.
4. Handy, C. (1989) *The Age of Unreason*. Hutchinson.
5. Osbourne, D. and Gaebler, T. (1992) *Reinventing Government*. New York: Addison Wesley.
6. Schumacher, E. (1973) *Small is Beautiful*. Abacus.
7. Osbourne, D. and Gaebler, T. (1992) *Reinventing Government*. New York: Addison Wesley.
8. Jones, J.H. (1988) *Making it Happen*. Collins.

INDEX